MW01609733

1000 FACTS ON

INSECTS

First published by Bardfield Press in 2005

Bardfield Press is an imprint of
Miles Kelly Publishing Ltd
Bardfield Centre, Great Bardfield, Essex, CM7 4SL

2 4 6 8 10 9 7 5 3 1

Editorial Director
Belinda Gallagher

Editorial Assistants
Amanda Askew, Hannah Todd

Picture Researcher
Liberty Newton

Designed and Packaged
Cyber Media (India) Ltd

Cover Designer
Tom Slemmings

Production Manager
Estela Boulton

Indexer
Helen Snaith

British Library Cataloguing-in-Publication Data
A catalogue record for this book is available from the British Library

ISBN 1–84236–523-1

Printed in China

www.mileskelly.net - info@mileskelly.net

1000 FACTS ON
INSECTS

Edited by Barbara Taylor

Contents

Key

Insect world

Ants, bees and wasps

Butterflies and moths

Flies, beetles and bugs

Cockroaches, crickets and grasshoppers

Other insects

Contents

Evolution

- **Insects** are small animals that belong to a class called Insecta. They are part of the phylum called Arthropoda.
- **Arthropods** include crustaceans (crabs and their relatives), myriapods (centipedes and millipedes), and arachnids (spiders, mites and scorpions), as well as insects.
- **The study of insects** is known as entomology.
- **Entomologists** have divided all the insects discovered so far into 32 groups or orders.
- **New species** of insects are constantly evolving as insects adapt themselves to their living conditions.

   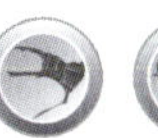  

◀ *Trapped in sticky tree resin millions of years ago, this delicate insect was beautifully preserved as the soft resin turned into hard amber.*

- **Some species of insects,** such as dragonflies or stoneflies, are so successful at surviving that they have not changed much over millions of years.
- **Fossils of insects** are sometimes preserved in the rocks. These fossils are often only fragments of various insect body parts.
- **It is difficult to find** insect fossils because the soft bodies of insects decay quickly and do not become fossilized.
- **Some whole insects** were trapped and fossilized in amber (pine tree resin).
- **The oldest fossils** of tiny wingless insects were found to be 380 million years old.

◀ *Insects were the first creatures on Earth to fly, more than 350 million years ago. Today, they are the only invertebrates (animals without backbones) that are able to fly.*

Insect fact file

- **There are over** one million different species of insects, compared to just one human species.
- **Insects are successful survivors** because of their powerful exoskeletons, their ability to fly and their minute size.
- **Some insects** can fly for long distances. Some butterflies migrate thousands of kilometres to avoid bad weather.
- **Cockroaches** have been living on Earth for around 300 million years. Today's cockroaches look very similar to those living hundreds of millions of years ago.
- **Insects** serve as the largest source of food for other animals.
- **Fairyflies** are the smallest insects in the world. They are only 0.2 mm – that is the size of a full stop.
- **Scientists discovered** the fossils of a dragonfly that lived 300 million years ago. It had a wingspan as big as a seagull.
- **People have domesticated** silkworms for so long that these insects do not exist in the wild anymore.

▲ *Cockroaches are so good at surviving that they have not needed to change for millions of years. They survived the dinosaurs and the Ice Ages and are still successful insects today.*

- **Insects are cold-blooded** animals, so their growth and development depends upon how hot or cold the weather is.
- **Scientists have developed 'insect robots'** that copy the agility of real insects. These robots are used to explore dangerous areas, such as minefields and the surface of other planets. Robots are not nearly as agile as real insects, but mimic the way they move.

▲ *Together, moths and butterflies, such as this swallowtail butterfly, make up one of the largest groups of insects. There are ten times more moths than butterflies.*

Insect firsts

- **Insects made the first paper**! Paper wasps chew the bark of some plants and add saliva to make a type of paper, occasionally adding sand particles for hardness. This 'paper' is used for building nests.
- **Insects such as the dragonfly** were the first ever fliers on Earth.
- **Dragonflies** are known to hover, like modern day helicopters, over their prey.
- **Insects were the first** animals to use sound as a means of communication. Bees use buzzing sounds to warn about danger, indicate the presence of food and convey various other information.
- **Cicadas and crickets** have been captured and reared by humans for the beautiful sound they can produce.
- **Insects were** the first to 'domesticate' other animals. Ants 'tame' larvae of certain butterflies and aphids and extract a type of sugary liquid called honeydew from them.
- **Dragonflies were familiar** with the idea of 'fast food' long before humans! They hold prey with their legs and eat it while flying.

▲ *Butterflies evolved when flowering plants were beginning to spread over the land and they were among the first pollinating insects.*

- **Termites** made the first ever colonies with the inhabitants engaged in different 'professions'. There are queens, soldiers and workers in termite colonies.

- **Insects used** the techniques of camouflage and ambush for defence and attack long before humans used them in military operations.

▼ *Termites built the first insect skyscrapers – towers of baked mud and saliva that are home to millions of termites. The large white queen lives in a special royal chamber while other chambers are used for rearing the young or storing food.*

FASCINATING FACT

Insects were the first doctors! Some insects produce toxins to combat and treat infections and diseases that occur in their bodies.

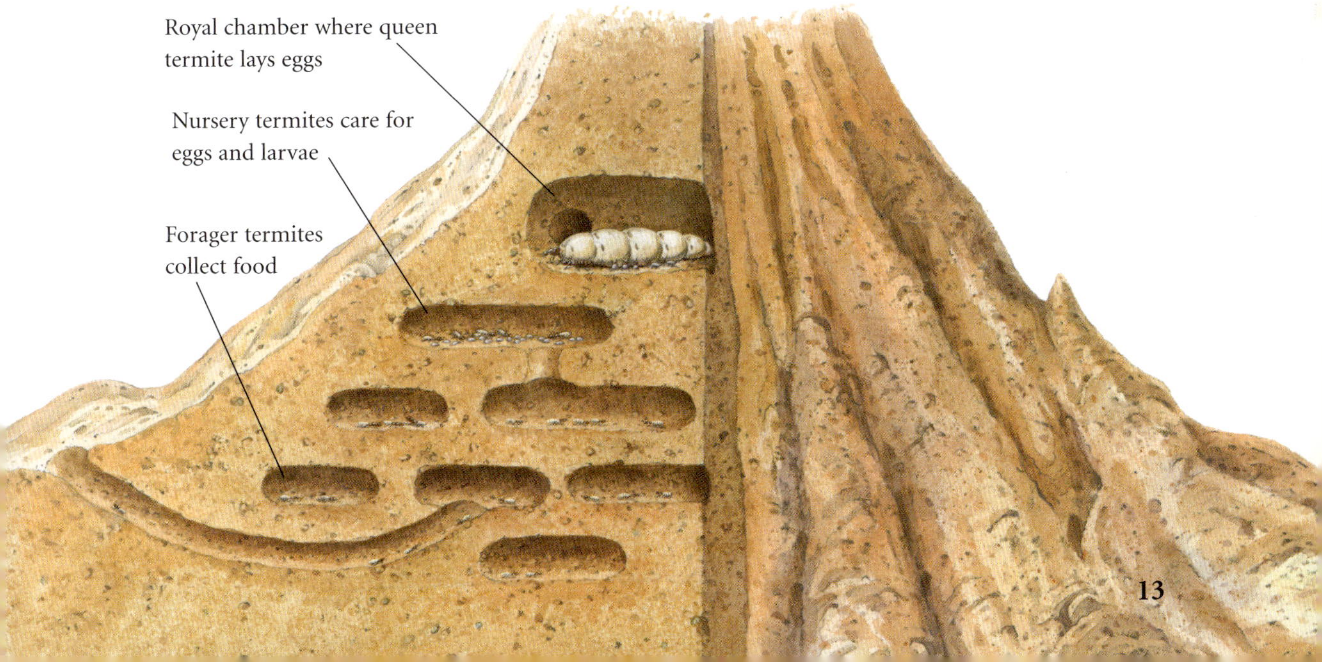

Insects and people

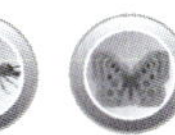

- **Insects were always** of great importance to human civilizations. People rear insects such as silkworms and honeybees to obtain important materials from them, such as silk, honey and wax.
- **Archaeologists** have discovered prehistoric cave paintings that show scenes of honey collection and the extraction of honey from beehives.
- **Japanese Samurai** warriors painted intricate butterfly patterns on weapons and flags to symbolize nobility.
- **Many stories**, songs and poems have been written about different insects in different cultures of the world.
- **Many insects**, such as mosquitoes and bed bugs, feed on human blood.
- **Many people eat** insects, such as termites, cicadas, leafcutter ants and water bugs, and consider them to be delicacies.
- **Deadly diseases** such as the Bubonic plague were transmitted to humans from tiny insects such as fleas, and caused millions of deaths.
- **Doctors** used to insert maggots in wounds to eat dead flesh and disinfect the wounds by killing bacteria.
- **Many insects feed** on agricultural pests and help farmers.
- **Some insects** can be pests and can destroy crops and fields and cause serious damage.

◀ *People began to domesticate bees about 3000 years ago. Today, most domesticated honeybees are kept in beehives containing removable frames. The bees store honey in the upper frames, which the beekeeper removes to harvest the honey.*

Sacred insects

...FASCINATING FACT...
Honeybees were believed to be the tears of the Egyptian Sun-god, Ra.

▲ *Images of scarab beetles were often carved on ancient Egyptian precious stones and jewellery. The carvings were thought to bring good luck and ward off evil.*

- **Ancient Egyptians** worshipped an array of beetles and other creepy crawlies, such as centipedes and scorpions.
- **The scarab or the dung beetle** was associated with the creator-god, Atum. This beetle was believed to have come into being by itself, from a ball of dung.
- **The jewel bug** has wings of metallic green, purple and golden colours. It is another insect revered by the ancient Egyptians.
- **Egyptians used amulets** with motifs of insects, such as locusts, beetles and flies, for good luck.
- **Egyptians believed** that honey could protect them from evil spirits.
- **Motifs of butterflies** have been discovered on ancient tombs and jewellery.
- **Some Moslems believe** that a praying mantis in the praying posture offers prayers towards Mecca.
- **Tiny black ants** are revered by some Hindus in India.
- **The ancient Chinese** regarded cicadas as a symbol of immortality and rebirth.

Anatomy

▶ *This diagram of a honeybee shows the main parts of an insect's body. A honeybee has two pairs of wings.*

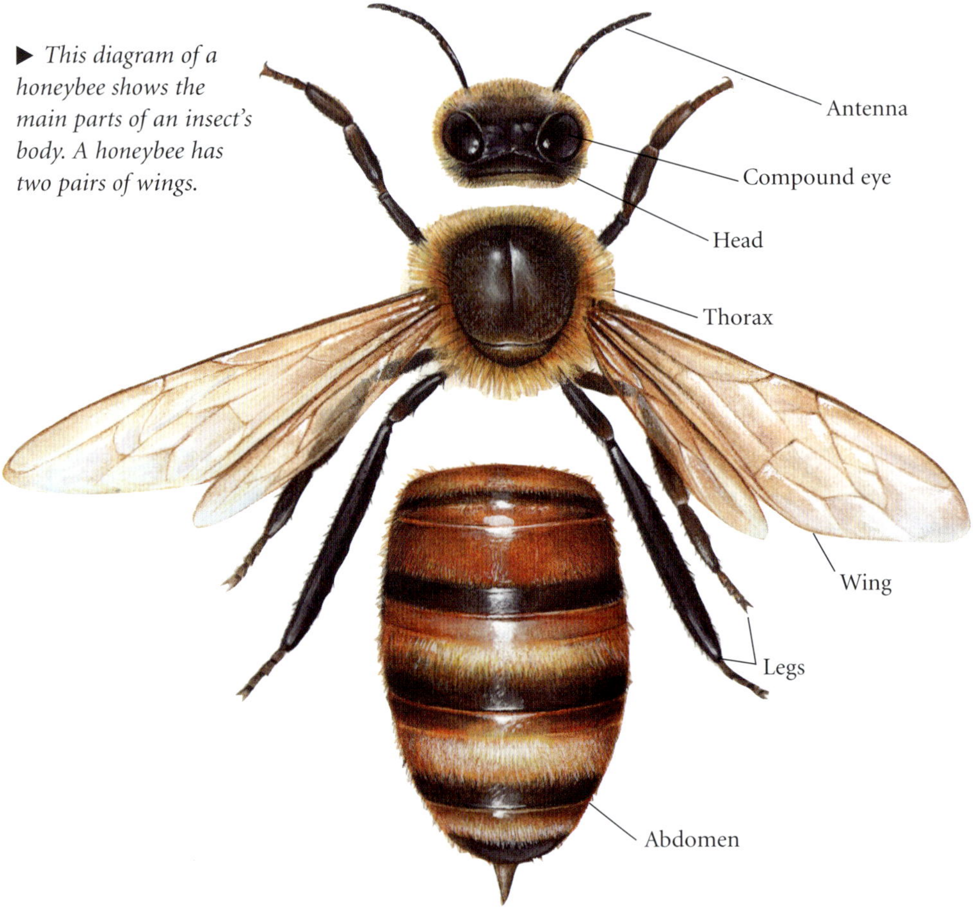

Antenna

Compound eye

Head

Thorax

Wing

Legs

Abdomen

- **The segmented body of an insect** is divided into three parts: head, thorax (middle section) and abdomen (rear section).
- **All insects have six legs** that are joined to the thorax. They usually have either one or two pairs of wings, which are also joined to the thorax.
- **Insects have** an exoskeleton, which is a strong outer skeleton that protects the insect's body.
- **The muscles** and delicate organs of insects are enclosed and protected within this exoskeleton.
- **Two antennae** on the insects head are used to sense smell, touch and sound.
- **The head** also contains mouthparts that are adapted to different feeding methods, such as chewing, biting, stabbing and sucking.
- **The digestive and reproductive systems** of insects are contained in the abdomen.
- **Insects have an open circulatory system** without lots of tubes for carrying blood. The heart of an insect is a simple tube that pumps greenish-yellow blood all over the body.
- **Insects breathe** through special openings on the side of the body called spiracles.
- **Insects have a tiny brain**, which is just a collection of nerve cells fused together. The brain sends signals to control all the other organs in the body.

Moulting

- **Moulting** is the shedding of the hard exoskeleton periodically because it does not stretch as the insect grows bigger. All insects moult during the early stages of their life.
- **To moult**, insects swallow a lot of air or water or use blood pressure to expand their body. The exoskeleton splits and the insect emerges.
- **A soft new exoskeleton** is exposed when the insect gets rid of its old one. The new exoskeleton is bigger in size and allows the insect to expand.
- **The new** exoskeleton hardens and becomes darker in colour.
- **Insects normally** moult five to ten times in a lifetime, depending on their species.
- **A silverfish** can moult up to 60 times in a lifetime.
- **The larval stage** between moults is known as an instar.
- **Moulting takes a long time** and the insect is vulnerable to predatory attacks during this period. Most insects moult in secluded areas.
- **Other animals**, such as snakes and spiders, also moult in order to grow.

FASCINATING FACT

A caterpillar grows about 2000 times bigger than its size at the time of its birth. If a 3 kg human baby grew at the same rate, the baby would weigh as much as a bus in a month.

▲ *A young adult dragonfly emerges during its final moult. After resting, it will pump blood into its short crumpled wings to spread them out to their full adult size.*

Defence

- **Insects use** different strategies apart from camouflage and mimicry to protect themselves from predators.
- **Some caterpillars** and larvae have special glands that secrete poison when they are attacked. Predatory birds soon learn to avoid them.
- **Stick insects and weevils** are known to 'play dead' when attacked. They simply keep very still and the attacker leaves the insects alone because most predators do not eat dead prey.
- **Ants, bees and wasps** can deliver painful stings to an attacker. These insects pump in venom and cause pain and irritation.
- **Some butterflies**, such as the monarch butterfly, are poisonous and cause the attacking bird to vomit if it eats the butterfly.
- **Insects, such as katydids**, shed their limbs if an attacker grabs them by the leg. This phenomenon is known as autotomy.
- **The bombardier beetle** has special glands, which can spray boiling hot poisonous fluids at an attacker.
- **Moths, grasshoppers and mantids** suddenly show the bright colours on their hind wings to startle a predator. These are called flash colours.
- **Stink glands** present in some bugs release obnoxious and repelling smells that predators cannot tolerate.

...FASCINATING FACT...

When alarmed, ants raise their abdomen. This sends a signal to other ants in the colony, and all the other ants raise their abdomens too.

▲ *This katydid could escape from the formidable claws of a desert scorpion by shedding a leg and flying away.*

Camouflage and mimicry

- **Insects use certain defence strategies**, such as camouflage and mimicry, to protect themselves from predators. Killer insects sometimes use the same strategies to catch their prey.
- **Some insects cleverly hide** themselves by blending in with their surroundings. This is known as camouflage.
- **Some harmless insects mimic** (imitate) harmful insects in appearance and behaviour. This fools predators into leaving them alone.
- **Hoverflies** have yellow-and-black stripes on their bodies, which makes them resemble stinging insects called wasps or hornets. Predators avoid the harmless hoverflies, assuming them to be wasps or hornets.
- **The larvae of some butterflies** resemble bird droppings, or even soil.
- **Stick insects and praying mantids** appear to be the twigs and leaves of plants. Predators often miss out on a possible meal because these insects blend into their environment very well. Even the pupae of some butterflies look like twigs.
- **Monarch butterflies** are bitter-tasting and poisonous, so birds do not eat them. Viceroy butterflies have orange and black wings similar those of monarch butterflies. Birds avoid viceroy butterflies because they think that they are poisonous as well.
- **Some moths imitate** dangerous wasps and bees in behaviour and sound. Their buzz startles predators, which leave them alone.

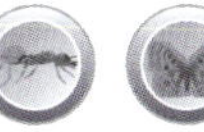

- **Adults and caterpillars** of some moths and butterflies have large eyelike spots to scare away predatory birds.
- **The velvet ant is actually a wasp**. It resembles an ant and can easily attack ant nests with this disguise.

▼ *The hornet moth has transparent wings and a yellow-and-black striped body, making it look like a large wasp called a hornet. It even behaves like a hornet when it flies. Predators, such as birds, avoid hornet moths because they look as if they might sting.*

Stings

- **Insects that belong** to the Hymenopteran order, such as ants, bees and wasps, are the most familiar stinging insects.
- **A stinging insect** has special organs that secrete venom (poison) and a sharp sting or teeth to inject venom into the victim.
- **The venom** can have a paralyzing effect on the prey. It can also damage tissues and cause pain. Hornet venom is the most potent.

▼ *A honeybee's jagged sting is a modified egg-laying tool, so only female bees can sting. Male bees do not have the necessary equipment at the end of their abdomen.*

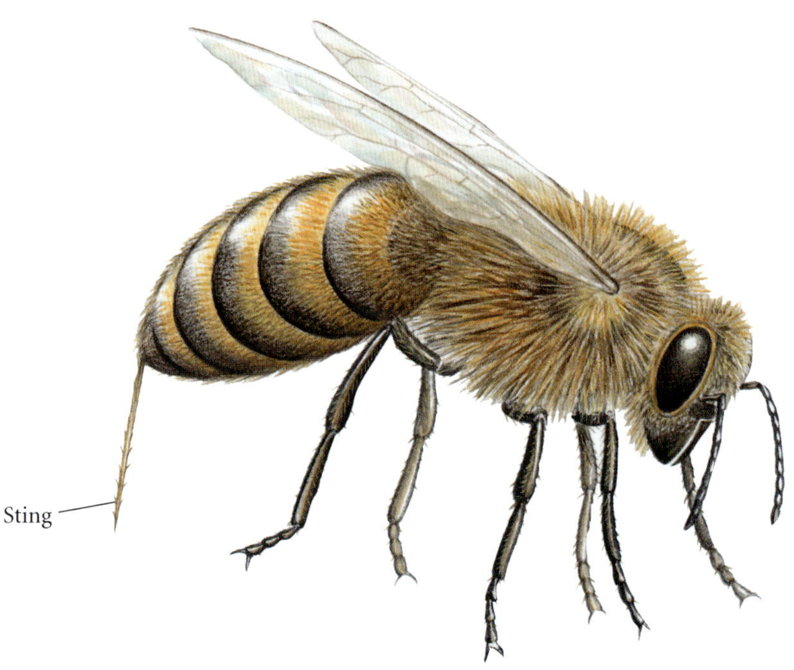

- **Insect venom** consists of enzymes, proteins and chemicals known as alkaloids.
- **Some insects**, such as mosquitoes, do not sting. They puncture the skin surface in order to suck up blood. Such insects can spread various diseases, such as malaria.
- **Insects sting** for two purposes: to catch prey and to defend themselves from predators.
- **Honeybees sting only once** and die soon after that. Their jagged stings remain stuck in their victim's skin, which tears out the honeybee's insides.
- **Wasps sting** their victims many times over because their stings are smooth and can be pulled out of the victims and used again.
- **Ants normally sting** as well as bite. They inject formic acid when they sting.

...FASCINATING FACT...

Ant venom glands have evolved to produce a chemical called pheromones, which the ants use to communicate.

Habitats

- **Insects have adapted** themselves to survive in almost every habitat on Earth, including some with extreme climates.
- **Entomologists** have discovered certain species of insect that live on volcanic lava and others that survive in cold polar regions.
- **Most insects live** in tropical regions where the warm temperatures are most suitable for their growth and development.
- **Insects can live in the freshwater** of ponds, lakes, streams, rivers, and even muddy pools and small waterholes.
- **Some insect species** can live very deep underwater while others need to come to the surface to breathe in air.
- **Many insects lay their eggs** in water and their larvae thrive underwater. These insects fly out to live in the air when they become adults.
- **Some insects**, such as the larvae of house-flies, live on different food materials.
- **Some insects** can survive on the surface of ponds of crude oil. They feed on other insects that fall in the oil.
- **Some insects can survive** on various man-made food sources, such as glue, paint, clothes and paper. They make their homes in our homes.

▶ *Temperate woodlands are home to a rich variety of insects because of the range of food and shelter available. The numbers and species of insect living in woodlands vary with the seasons and the types of trees dominating the woodlands.*

FASCINATING FACT

Around 97 percent of the insect world lives on the land or in freshwater. Very few insects can survive in the sea.

Capsid bug

Shield bug

Flower bug

Fruit fly

Furniture beetle

Winter survival

Peacock butterfly

Ladybird

Squash beetle

▲ *Hibernating insects search for safe hiding places in which to survive the winter. Peacock butterflies have a chemical 'antifreeze' that helps to stop their body fluids freezing during very cold weather.*

- **Insects use** various methods to survive severe winters. Most species go into a deep sleep for a long time called hibernation. Their body temperature falls to just above that of the surroundings and vital body processes slow down.

- **Some insects spend winters** in a dormant state known as diapause. They stop developing and growing and their body processes slow down. Diapause is most common among moth pupae.
- **Some insects** spend the winter in galls, or swellings, that they cause on plants. Galls provide these insects with food and shelter.
- **Beetles and ants** may burrow deep furrows in the ground and keep themselves warm inside them.
- **Ladybirds** cluster together in huge numbers when they hibernate.
- **Some butterflies and moths** survive harsh winters by hibernating in tree holes, caves or even garden sheds. They may hibernate for months before emerging in spring or summer.
- **Some insects** survive the winter as eggs, which only start to develop the following spring.
- **Some species of beetle** store fat in their bodies to keep themselves warm.
- **Some insects replace the water content** in their body with glycerol, which works as an antifreeze.
- **Honeybees stay inside** their hives during cold weather and raise the temperature by vibrating their wings or clustering together to keep warm.

Migration

- **Insects migrate** across great distances in search of suitable living and breeding conditions. They often migrate when the weather gets colder or hotter or when food becomes scarce.

. . . FASCINATING FACT . . .

Migrating butterflies such as the painted lady do not return to their home ground but the next generation does.

- **Migrating insects may land in** some places and lay a large number of eggs before moving on.

▼ *Migrating locusts grow broader shoulders and longer wings to help them fly fast and for long distances. A swarm of locusts may contain thousands of millions of individuals and fly as much as 3200 km in a year.*

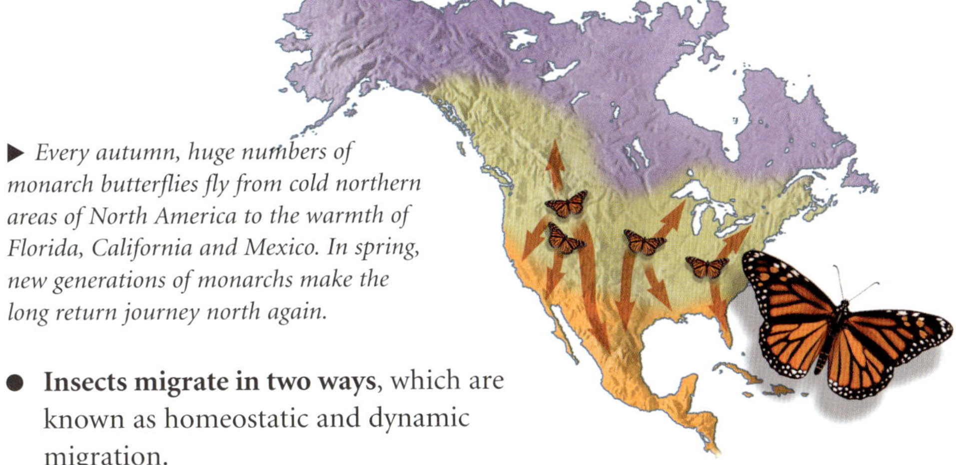

▶ *Every autumn, huge numbers of monarch butterflies fly from cold northern areas of North America to the warmth of Florida, California and Mexico. In spring, new generations of monarchs make the long return journey north again.*

- **Insects migrate in two ways**, which are known as homeostatic and dynamic migration.
- **Homeostatic migration** is when insects pass through a defined path and also return the same way. In dynamic migration, insects depend upon the wind or tides to decide their path of movement.
- **Monarch butterflies** are known to migrate across continents. These butterflies can cover a distance of more than 3000 km.
- **Butterflies may travel** in huge groups of millions of butterflies. Most of the older butterflies cannot withstand the journey and die on the way.
- **Pilots have spotted** migrating butterflies at an altitude of 1200 m.
- **Locusts migrate** across farmlands in large swarms in search of greener pastures.
- **Army ants** do not build permanent nests because they constantly migrate in search of food.

Ants

- **Ants are one of the most successful insects** on Earth. There are more than 9000 different species.
- **The study of ants** is known as myrmecology. People sometimes rear ants in elaborate ant farms.
- **Ants belong** to an order of insects known as Hymenoptera. Bees and wasps also belong to this group.
- **Entomologists** believe that ants evolved from wasps millions of years ago.

...FASCINATING FACT...
Birds allow ants to crawl on their bodies and spray them with formic acid. Known as anting, this gets rid of parasites from their feathers.

- **Ants are social insects**, which live in huge colonies. These colonies consist of the queen ant, female workers and male ants.
- **In ant colonies**, the different ants divide themselves into groups that perform various tasks. Some ants are cleaners, some take care of the young ones while others gather food or defend the nest.
- **Ants are intelligent** insects. Experts have calculated that an ant brain can function as fast as a powerful computer.
- **An ant can lift a weight** that is 20 to 50 times more than its own body weight.
- **Ants spray formic acid** on predators to defend themselves. People once obtained formic acid by boiling ants.

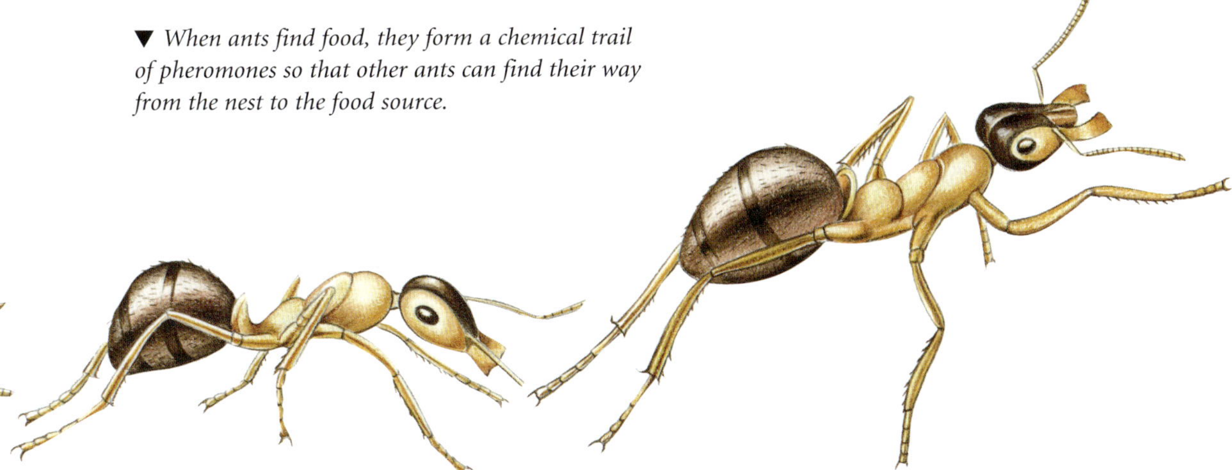

▼ *When ants find food, they form a chemical trail of pheromones so that other ants can find their way from the nest to the food source.*

More ants

- **Most ants** live in anthills that are made of mounds of soil, sand and sticks but some nest in trees.
- **Anthills consist** of different chambers and tunnels. Each chamber is used for different purposes, such as food storage, nurseries for the young or resting areas.
- **Not all ants** live in anthills. Army ants are nomadic in nature. They carry their eggs and young ones along with them while travelling and set up temporary camps.
- **The queen ant** is the largest ant in the colony. When she matures, the queen ant flies off in search of a suitable place to build a new colony.

▼ *Tailor, or weaver, ants make nests out of leaves or similar materials sewed together with silk produced by the larvae.*

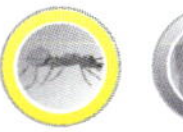

- **Queen ants** nip off their wings once they find a place to breed. Smaller worker ants also have wings.
- **Worker ants** take good care of the eggs. At night, they carry the eggs into deep nest tunnels to protect them from cold. In the morning, the workers carry the eggs back to the surface to warm them.

◀ *Ants are very small insects, ranging in size from about 2 to 25 mm. A typical ant has a large head and a narrow 'waist' where the thorax joins the abdomen. The antennae have a distinctive bend so they look as if they have 'elbows'.*

- **Male ants die shortly** after mating with the queen ant.
- **Ants have two stomachs**. One stomach carries its own food while the other carries food that will be shared with other ants. This is called the crop.
- **Ants communicate** with the help of their feelers (antennae). They also leave scent trails behind them to let the other ants know where exactly to find the food source.
- **Each ant colony** has a unique smell that helps the members to identify each other. This also helps the ants to detect an intruder in the nest.

Army ant

- **Army ants constantly migrate** in search of food. They can attack and enslave ants living in other colonies.
- **Army ants march** at night and stop to camp in the morning.
- **Nomadic in nature**, army ants do not build permanent nests.
- **Temporary nests** are formed by army ants while the queen lays her eggs. The ants cling onto each other and form the walls and chambers.
- **Army ants are voracious eaters.** They march in swarms of up to one million ants and eat almost 50,000 insects a day!
- **These ants eat insects, birds and small animals** that cross their path. Army ants can even eat a horse.
- **Army ants have simple and not compound eyes** like other ant species. However, worker army ants are blind.
- **Army ants have not evolved** (changed) much in the last 100 million years.
- **Some people allow** army ants to march into their homes and clear them of insects and other pests.

...FASCINATING FACT...
A queen army ant can lay up to 4 million eggs in one month.

▶ *The army ants of tropical America march in columns, just like real soldiers. To cross gaps, some of the ants form bridges with their bodies, allowing the rest of the army to swarm over the living bridge. The worker ants also link up to form chains that surround the queen and young.*

Leafcutter ant

- **Leafcutter ants** cut out bits of leaves from plants and carry them back to their underground nest.
- **Leafcutter ants cannot digest leaves**. These ants feed on a fungus that is specially grown by them.
- **The cut leaf pieces** are used to fertilize special fungus farms that are grown inside the ant nest. There can be numerous fungus farms in a single nest.
- **Leafcutter ants** are normally found in tropical rainforests.
- **A queen leafcutter ant** can produce about 15 million offspring during her lifetime.
- **Leafcutter ants divide** themselves into workers and soldiers. The biggest ants are soldiers, which protect the nest.
- **Small worker ants** take care of the young and manage the nest, while the bigger worker ants go out and cut pieces of leaves for the fungus farms.
- **In some species** of leafcutter ant, tiny workers ride on the pieces of snipped leaves. They protect the larger workers from flies that try to lay their eggs on them.
- **Leafcutter ants are eaten** in some cultures. They are a rich source of protein.
- **Leafcutter ants do not sting**, but they can bite.

▶ *Leafcutter ants in Central and South American rainforests often cut leaves 50 to 200 m away from their nest. Each leaf fragment can take two or three minutes to cut and is many times to size of the tiny ant.*

Weaver ant

▶ *Weaver ants joining leaves together to make their nest.*

- **Weaver ants** build their colonies in the top of trees, using live green leaves.
- **The larvae of weaver ants** secrete a sticky silklike substance. Adult ants use the young larvae like glue sticks.
- **A team of adult worker weaver ants** holds two leaves together, while a single worker holding a larva runs through the edges and 'sews' them together. The worker ant holds the larva in its mandibles (mouthparts) and uses the silky secretion to stick the leaves together.

  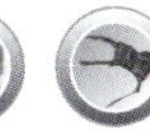  

- **A colony can contain** about 150 weaver nests in 20 different trees. The queen ant's nest is built in the centre of the colony. It is made with extra silk and is feathery in appearance.
- **The larger worker (soldier) ants** fiercely protect their nest, while the smaller workers take care of various chores inside the nest.
- **Weaver ants are carnivores** and feed on body fluids from small, soft bodied insects. Some species also feed on honeydew.
- **For 2000 years**, the Chinese have used weaver ants to control pest infestations in their crop fields.
- **Weaver ants do not sting** but they can inflict very painful bites if provoked. When they bite, weaver ants squirt formic acid into the wound, which causes even more pain.
- **Some caterpillars** and spiders camouflage themselves as weaver ants and attack weaver ant nests. The spiders may even smell like weaver ants.

...FASCINATING FACT...

Weaver ants are eaten in Eastern cultures. The oil extracted from these ants is often used as sweeteners in food items. The pupae are said to be creamy in taste. Adult ants have a lemony taste and are used to flavour rice!

Bees

- **There are approximately 20,000** species of bee. Many bees live alone but over 500 species are social and live in colonies.
- **Bees are small** in size, ranging from 2 to 4 cm in length. They have hairs and a sting to protect them. The hairs also help them to collect pollen.
- **Bees are generally black or grey** in colour but can also be yellow, red, green or blue.
- **Bees feed on** pollen and nectar collected from flowers. Pollen contains protein and nectar provides energy.
- **Social bees secrete wax** to build their nests. A honeybee colony may contain 3000 to 40,000 bees depending on the species, the season and the locality. It consists of a single queen bee, female workers and male drones.
- **The male drones** do not have stings and their function is to mate with the queen bee. The queen lays about 600 to 700 eggs every day.
- **Bees have five eyes**. They have two compound eyes and three simple eyes, or ocelli. Bees cannot see red but they can see ultraviolet light, which is invisible to us.
- **A normal bee's lifespan** ranges from five to six weeks but a queen bee can live up to five years.
- **Bees communicate** with other bees about the distance, direction and quality or quantity of the food source through a unique combination of dance and sounds.
- **A honeybee attacks** either to protect itself or its colony. Once a bee stings, it leaves behind its sting and venom in the victim's body. As the bee pulls away from the victim, it dies when its organs are pulled out of its abdomen.

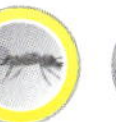

▲ *Honeybee workers crowd around their queen. The workers lick and stroke their queen to pick up powerful scents called pheromones, which pass on information about the queen and tell the workers how to behave.*

Bee behaviour

- **Bees have two kinds** of mouthparts. The first kind, found in honeybees, is adapted for sucking. The other kind is adapted for biting. This is found in carpenter bees.
- **The antennae** are the organs of touch and smell. Bees use their antennae to detect flower fragrances and to find nectar.
- **Bees can rarely distinguish** sweet and bitter tastes but can identify sour and salty tastes. Bees use their front legs, antennae and proboscis for tasting.
- **Bees have no ears**, but they can sense vibrations through their sensitive hairs.

▲ *Bees are important because they carry pollen from flower to flower so that seeds can grow. The bright colours of flowers and the nectar they produce encourages bees to visit them.*

- **Bees do not sleep at night**, although they remain motionless.
- **Wild bees nest underground** or in tree holes, caves or under houses. Honeybees also live in hives constructed by people.
- **Social bees** follow a hierarchical structure. They live in large colonies of queens, males and workers. The queen cell is structurally different from the worker cells. Males do not help in the organization and other activities of the colony.
- **When a colony** becomes overcrowded, some of the bees fly to a different location. This phenomenon is called swarming. It is a part of the annual life cycle of the bee colony.
- **A division of labour** exists among social bees. The queen bee lays eggs and male bees fertilize the queen bee. Worker bees perform various tasks, such as cleaning the cells, keeping the young warm and guarding them, feeding larvae, producing wax and collecting food for the colony.
- **The queen bee** secretes pheromones, which tell worker bees that she is alive and well and inhibit the development of worker bees into queens. Once she lays eggs, the fertilized eggs become female worker bees and the unfertilized eggs become male bees.

Bee nests

- **Social bees make complex nests**, which consist of a number of cells, often built in flat sheets called combs.
- **Social bees**, such as honeybees, bumblebees and stingless bees, make cells of wax. However, honeybees are the only species that makes prominent honeycombs. People sometimes keep honeybees in beehives for their honey.
- **Honeycombs** are made up of hexagonal cells and are divided into three main sections. The upper section is used for storing honey and the middle section for storing pollen. The lower section is used to house the eggs and young.
- **The hexagonal shape** of the honeycomb cells allows the maximum amount of honey to be stored and uses the least amount of wax.
- **Social bees use their nests** to raise their eggs, larvae and pupae, collectively called their brood. Some also use their nests to prepare and store honey for the winter.
- **Bees use 'bee glue' (propolis)**, a sticky tree resin, to strengthen and repair their nests.

▶ *A honeybee hive showing some of the cells used for storing pollen, honey eggs, or developing larvae.*

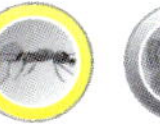

- **Bees use water** as a coolant to maintain an optimum temperature of 35° C in a beehive. They also flutter their wings to maintain the temperature at the correct level.
- **Male drones** have bigger cells than the female workers in a honeybee hive.
- **A bumblebee queen** builds her nest in a hole in the ground. She may use the abandoned nests of birds, mice, ants or termites.
- **Stingless bees build** saclike combs. They are made from a mixture of resin and wax called cerumen. The combs are held together by propolis in the hollows of trees, rocks and walls.

Honey

▲ *A natural honeycomb, showing the double layer of six-sided cells constructed by the bees to store honey. The honeycomb is used in the winter as food for the larvae and other members of the bee colony.*

- **Honey** is a natural, unrefined sweetener, which is an alternative to sugar.
- **Every 100 g** of honey provides 319 kcal of energy.
- **Bees collect** the nectar of flowers, and other plant secretions, and turn it into honey. It is then altered chemically into different types of sugars and stored in the comb cells.
- **The honey in a honeycomb** includes matured nectar, pollen, bee saliva and wax granules.
- **Honey mainly contains** moisture, sugars and minerals. Several trace elements, such as calcium, phosphorous, magnesium, iron, silica and vitamin C, are also present.
- **Honey is considered** to be the only source of food that has all the energy and protein reserves necessary to sustain life.
- **The colour and flavour** of honey depends upon the climate and the flowers from which the nectar has been collected.
- **Honey serves** as an important source of medicines because of its mild laxative, bactericidal, sedative, antiseptic and alkaline characteristics.

▲ *Stored honey keeps worker honeybees and their developing young alive during the long cold winters in temperate areas when other bee colonies die out.*

- **Honey extracted from wild beehives** can be dangerous if the nectar is obtained from poisonous flowers.
- **Honey** is used in a fluid medium in the preservation of the cornea (layer at the front of the eye).

Bumblebee

- **Bumblebees** are hairy, black, yellow or orange in colour and up to 25 mm long. They are most common in temperate regions and are less aggressive than other bees.
- **Bumblebees live** in small colonies of between 50 to 600 bees.

▲ *Bumblebees collect pollen from flowers in pollen baskets (long, stiff bristles) on their back legs. The bee combs the yellow pollen dust from its body and packs it tightly into the pollen baskets until they are full.*

- **Bumblebees build** their nests on the ground in rocky holes, grassy hollows or deserted rodent or bird nests. The chambers are spherical in shape with one exit. The cells inside are capsule shaped.
- **The queen bumblebee** lays her eggs in wax cups inside the nest. The wax is secreted by her abdominal glands.
- **Only the young queen bumblebees** survive the winter. The rest of the bees in the colony die.
- **Bumblebees regulate** their body temperature with the help of their body hair. The queens hibernate in the winter and come out in the spring to lay their eggs and start a new colony.
- **Bumblebees are low fliers** and move slowly around the flowers.
- **Bumblebees help** to pollinate plants, such as red clover. Their long tongue enables them to reach deep inside flowers.
- **In summer**, the bumblebee workers fan their wings to cool the developing young. The buzzing sound of fanning is so loud that it can be heard from a distance.

...FASCINATING FACT...

Bumblebees do not produce large quantities of honey. They store honey just for feeding themselves and their young.

Carpenter bee

▶ *A carpenter bee is about 20 to 25 mm long. It is not as hairy as a bumblebee, with short hairs on its abdomen or sometimes no hair at all.*

- **Carpenter bees** are named after their habit of drilling into wood for building nests.
- **Blue-black** or metallic in colour, carpenter bees resemble large bumblebees.

- **Carpenter bees are found** all over the world, especially in areas where woody plants flourish. They are common in forested regions of the tropics.
- **Carpenter bees are solitary** in nature and do not live in colonies.
- **Male carpenter bees** have white-coloured faces or white markings and females have black-coloured faces.
- **Males** do not have a sting but they do guard the nest. The females do have stings but are very docile and do not sting unless in danger.
- **Female carpenter bees** nest in their wooden tunnels. They prefer weathered, unpainted, bare wood. In these tunnels, carpenter bees drill holes, where they lay eggs in individual cells and store enough food for the larvae to grow. There is only a single entrance to each tunnel.
- **People take preventive measures**, such as spraying pesticides, to keep carpenter bees away from their home and gardens.

...FASCINATING FACT...

Adult carpenter bees hibernate during the winter. They remain in their wooden nest, surviving on stored honey and pollen.

Honeybee

► *Honeybees have a hairy thorax and an abdomen with orange-yellow rings separating the segments.*

- **Honeybees** are social insects. They live in large colonies and are the most popular species of bees.
- **Some well-known species** of honeybee are Italian bees, Carniolan (Slovenian) bees, Caucasian bees, German black bees and Africanized honeybees.
- **In a honeybee colony**, different groups of bees carry out different tasks. A colony is made up of a queen bee, female workers and male drones.
- **Queen bees** are sexually productive and responsible for laying eggs that develop into drones and worker bees.
- **Worker bees** have a sharp sting, pollen baskets, wax secreting glands and a honey sac for collecting honey. The wax is used to build sheets of cells called combs.
- **Worker bees build** the nest as well as collect pollen and nectar for food. They are also responsible for maintaining the nursery temperature at 34°C, which is ideal for hatching the eggs and rearing the larvae.
- **Drones** do not have a sting. Their sole function is to mate with the queen; they die after mating. During the winter, they are driven out by the workers to die.
- **Honeybees** are the biggest producers of honey. This is why they are the species most domesticated by humans.

- **Honeybees** have an amazing mode of communication among themselves – dancing. Dr Karl Von Frisch won the Nobel Prize for deciphering the bee dance.
- **Honeybees are susceptible** to various diseases and attacks by parasites. Parasite and virus attacks may cause paralysis in bees.

◀ *A honeybee has a long tongue to collect the nectar from flowers. The bee may visit up to 1000 flowers on just one collecting trip.*

Leaf-cutter bee

...FASCINATING FACT...

The average lifespan of a female leaf-cutter bee is two months and in this time, she lays 30 to 40 eggs.

▼ *A female leaf-cutter bee snips off a piece of leaf with her sharp, scissor-like jaws. She will roll up the leaf fragment and carry it between her legs as she flies back to her nest.*

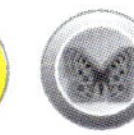

- **Leaf-cutter bees** are named after their habit of cutting pieces of leaf to make a protective casing for their eggs. They nest in the soil, hollow plant stems or woody tunnels.
- **Leaf-cutter bees are black** in colour with hair on their abdomen. This hair helps them collect pollen, unlike other bees, which collect pollen on their legs.
- **Most leaf-cutter bees** are solitary in nature. Females like to construct individual nests independently. Males are smaller than females and have hairy faces.
- **The female bee** builds her nest using semicircular leaf pieces for the side walls and circular pieces for the ends. Once the cell is ready, she stores pollen and honey inside, lays an egg and closes each cell with a perfectly fitted disk of cut leaf. Then she begins the sequence again until the entire nest is complete.
- **Individual female leaf-cutter bees** do all the work. They select the nesting place, construct cells, lay the eggs and rear the larvae.
- **Leaf-cutter bees** are docile in nature with a mild sting. They use the sting to defend themselves from attack.
- **They can harm plants** because of their habit of constructing nests with plant leaves. Their favourite plant is the rose plant.
- **Leaf-cutter bees help some plants**, such as alfalfa, with pollination. They do this by carrying the pollen from one plant to another.
- **Leaf-cutter bees** have many enemies, such as wasps, velvet ants and some species of blister beetle.

Wasps

▶ *This close-up of a wasp's head shows the large black compound eyes, which are good at detecting movement and can see certain colours. Wasps also have sharp, cutting jaws with jagged edges.*

- **Wasps belong** to the Hymenopteran order, as do bees and ants. They have a hard exoskeleton and their body is divided into head, thorax and abdomen. They have four transparent wings and two compound eyes.
- **Wasps are solitary** as well as social insects. Social wasps live in huge colonies while solitary wasps live alone. There are about 17,000 species of wasps, but only about 1500 species are social.
- **Wasp nests** can be simple or complex. Some nests are just burrows in the ground while others are built with mud and twigs and can have many cells and tunnels.
- **Each nest** has at least one queen wasp as well as workers and males.
- **Not all wasps build nests**. Some wasps such as cuckoo wasps, lay eggs in the nests of other bees and other wasps.

...FASCINATING FACT...
When disturbed, female wasps can sting.

- **Other species of wasp** lay their eggs in stems, leaves, fruits and flowers instead of building nests.
- **Adult wasps feed** on nectar, and fruit and plant sap while the larvae feed on insects.
- **Many species of wasp** are parasitic in nature, which means that they live part of their lives as parasites inside other insects. The larvae of such wasps feed on other insects and sometimes eat plant tissues.
- **Wasps are helpful** for controlling pests, such as caterpillars.

▲ *Wasps do not store food in their nest as the cells face downwards and are open at the bottom. The queen wasp has to glue her eggs inside the cells to stop them falling out.*

Gall wasp

- **Gall wasps** are small parasitic insects that feed on plants.
- **These insects** are named after their habit of causing the formation of a tumour-like growth in plants, known as galls.
- **Galls are an abnormal growth** of plant tissues and leaves. Some of them look like greenish apples or berries on leaves.
- **Galls are formed** when a female gall wasp injects her eggs into a plant. When the eggs hatch, the larvae release some chemicals, which causes the plant to cover them with soft tissues in the form of a gall.
- **Galls can be** either spongy or hollow inside.
- **Gall wasp larvae** feed on the gall and pupate inside it. Adult gall wasps emerge from the gall either by boring a hole or by bursting it through the surface.

▲ *Gall wasps are usually about 2 to 8 mm long. Their shiny abdomen is oval in shape and their wings have few veins.*

- **Different types of galls**, such as leaf, flower, seed and stem galls, are caused by different species of gall wasp.
- **A gall is like a nursery** for one or more species of gall wasp.
- **A species of gall wasp**, known as a fig wasp, causes the formation of seed galls inside wild figs and in the process, pollinates them. No other insect pollinates wild figs.
- **Gall wasps are very selective** about the plants on which they lay their eggs. For instance, some gall wasps lay their eggs on figs, while others prefer roses.

▼ *Female fig wasps lay their eggs on some of the flowers inside immature figs. The eggs develop into larvae, pupae and adults. Adult females emerge and fly off to find other figs in which to lay their eggs. The wingless male wasps die without ever leaving the fig.*

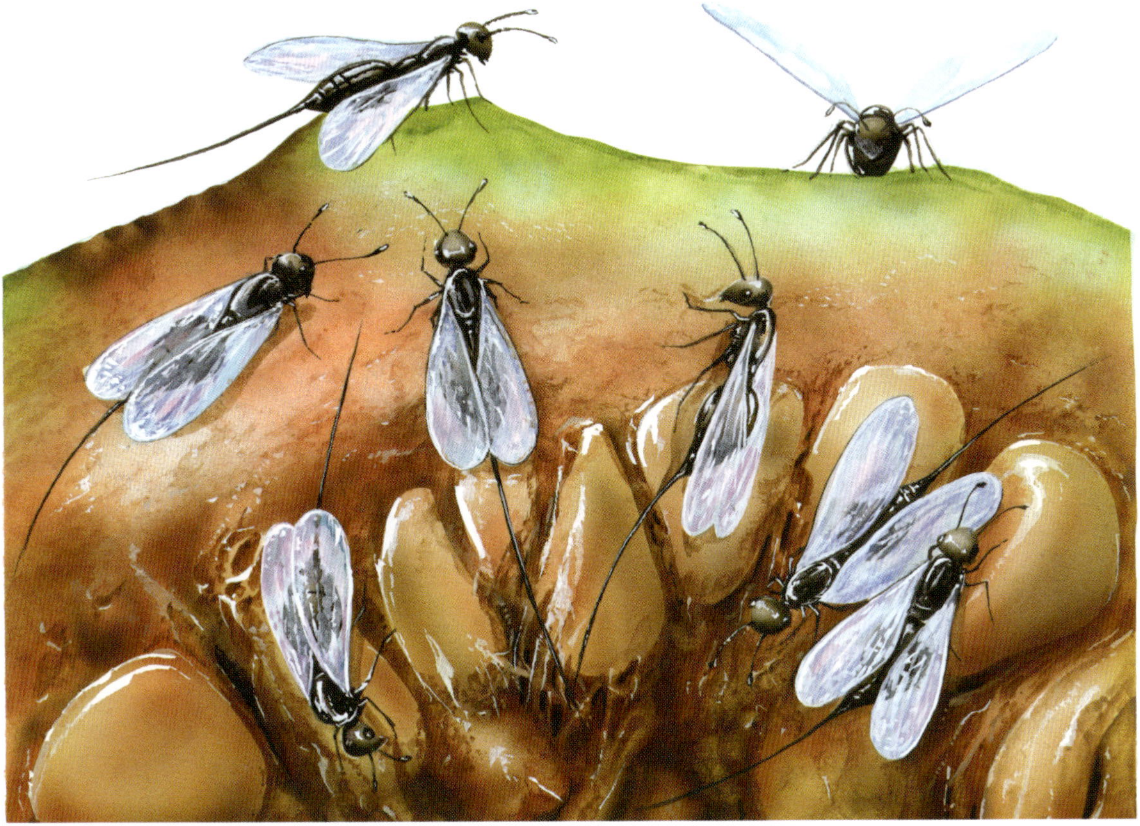

Hornet

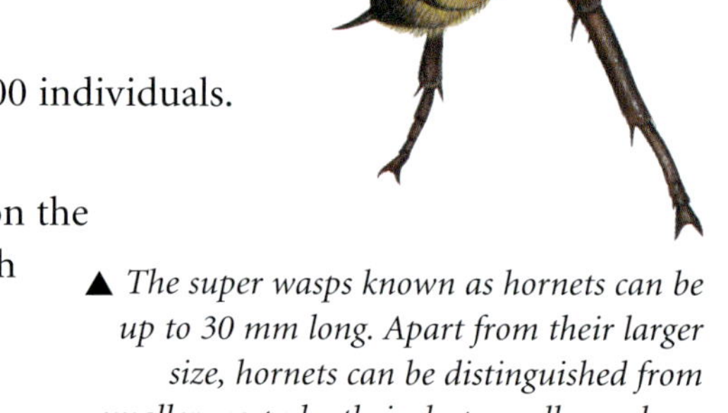

▲ *The super wasps known as hornets can be up to 30 mm long. Apart from their larger size, hornets can be distinguished from smaller wasps by their deeper yellow colour.*

- **Hornets** belong to the order Hymenoptera and the Vespidae family. They have dark brown and yellow stripes all over their body.
- **Hornets are known** for their ferocious nature and painful sting. They are huge, robust wasps and are social in nature.
- **Social hornets** form huge colonies that can contain about 25,000 individuals.
- **Hornets can build** their nest anywhere – at a height or even on the ground. They insulate their nests with layers of 'paper'.
- **These insects chew plant fibre** and mix it with saliva to form a papery paste, which they use to build nests. The nest is spherical, with an entrance at the bottom and is divided into many tiers inside. These tiers have hexagonal cells, in which the young ones are raised.
- **Hornets build** the largest nests of all wasps. A hornet nest can be 122 cm long and 91 cm in circumference.
- **Hornet colonies die** out in one year. No member of the colony survives the winter except the female hornets that have mated.

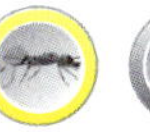

- **Abandoned hornet** nests provide shelter to other insects during the winter.
- **Some insects** have stripes, which resemble those of hornets. These ward off predators, which mistake harmless insects for hornets.

FASCINATING FACT

Hornets are known to chase their tormentors. Hence the saying 'never stir a hornet's nest'.

▼ *Although hornets are very protective of their nest, they are far less likely to sting than smaller wasps. A hornet's nest can be as large as a basketball and is constructed in hollow trees, under roof eaves, porches, outbuildings or even gardens.*

Paper wasp

- **Paper wasps are reddish-brown** in colour and have yellow stripes on their body.
- **They are social insects** and live in small colonies of 20 to 30 insects. After the queen wasp mates, she builds a nest with a material quite similar to papier mache (paper pulp). It is made of six-sided cells covered in layers of paper. The nests are mostly built in the spring.

▲ *The small nest entrance is easy to defend from other insects and also helps the wasps to control the humidity and temperature inside the nest.*

...FASCINATING FACT...

The Chinese were inspired by the humble paper wasp to invent paper.

- **Paper wasps chew** plant fibre, which they mix with their saliva to build their nests.
- **A few queen paper wasps** build a nest together. The most powerful queen dominates and leads the colony, while the others become workers.
- **Some paper wasp nests** look like inverted umbrellas, which is why these insects are also known as 'umbrella wasps'.
- **The subordinate** queen wasps are called joiners. Sometimes, a joiner manages to overpower the reigning queen. She becomes the new queen while the original queen becomes a worker.
- **Unlike other wasps**, bees and ants, queen paper wasps closely resemble the worker wasps.
- **Adult paper wasps** feed only on nectar while the young larvae feed on chewed insects.
- **Sometimes**, army ants invade paper wasp nests and destroy the entire colony.

▶ *This Costa Rican paper wasp is starting to build her nest under a leaf. She will use her antennae to measure the size of the cells.*

Parasitic wasps

▼ *Ichneumon wasps are mainly parasites of butterfly and moth larvae but many are hyperparasites. The ichneumon larvae grow and develop inside their living host, only killing the host when they are nearly fully grown and ready to pupate.*

- **Parasitic wasps lay their eggs** inside other wasps, spiders and insects, such as bees, caterpillars and aphids.
- **Female parasitic wasps** inject their eggs into the body of their host with the help of an ovipositor, or egg-laying tube. Once the eggs hatch, the larvae literally eat their way out of the host.
- **Parasitic wasps** can lay as many as 3000 eggs inside a single host insect.
- **Some parasitic wasps**, such as chalcid and braconid wasps, are known for infesting moth and butterfly caterpillars. They are helpful for controlling the caterpillar populations in crop fields.
- **Some very tiny wasps** specialize in parasitizing insect eggs. These eggs have the ability to multiply into many cells and almost 150 individual wasps of the same sex can hatch from a single egg.
- **The smallest insect**, the fairyfly, is an egg parasite wasp. A fairyfly measures only about 0.2 mm.
- **A parasitic wasp can be infested** by a smaller parasitic wasp, which in turn can be infested by another wasp. This phenomenon is known as hyperparasitism. This is similar to a large box containing a small box that contains yet another smaller box inside it and so on.
- **Unlike** other social wasps and bees, parasitic wasps do not sting.
- **Aphids** that serve as hosts for parasitic wasps appear puffy and hard. They die once the wasp larvae are ready to pupate. Such aphids are known as aphid mummies.
- **Parasitic wasps** are useful to us because their normal hosts are pest insects.

Velvet ant

- **These wasps** resemble huge hairy ants, which is why they are known as velvet ants.
- **Velvet ants are usually** red, brown or black in colour.
- **Found** in dry areas, velvet ants are densely covered with long, whitish hair. When it is too hot to venture outside, velvet ants burrow underground or climb into plants.

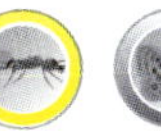

- **Male velvet ants** have wings and cannot sting. Females, on the other hand, do not have wings and can sting. They move about on the ground like ants and their sting can be quite painful.
- **Velvet ants** have a tough outer covering, which protects them against bee and wasp stings.
- **Female velvet ants** move very swiftly and are often found busily searching for the burrows of solitary bees and wasps.
- **Velvet ants lay eggs** in the nests of bees and other wasps and are parasitic in nature.
- **The larva of the velvet ant** emerges before the eggs of its host hatch. It eats its host's eggs as well as its larvae.
- **Velvet ants make** a squeaky noise if they are attacked or captured.
- **The sting** of the velvet ant is so powerful that people believed it could kill a cow. This, however, is not true.

◀ *The females lay their eggs in bumblebee nests and the velvet ant larvae feed on the bee larvae.*

Butterfly life-style

- **Butterflies do not have a mouth** or teeth to chew or break their food into small pieces. Instead they have a long strawlike structure called a proboscis under their head, which helps them suck nectar and other juices.

▲ *A butterfly drinking nectar from a flower using its proboscis.*

- **A butterfly's wings** are covered with microscopic scales, which overlap like roof tiles.
- **Butterflies are usually active** during the day and fly only in the daytime. Some tropical butterflies also fly at night.
- **Butterflies pass through four different stages of development**, also called metamorphosis. An adult butterfly lays eggs on plants. The egg hatches into a caterpillar or larva. The caterpillar develops into a pupa or chrysalis. The pupa finally matures into a butterfly.
- **The caterpillars grow 27,000 times bigger** than their original size when they first emerge from the eggs. They shed their skin from time to time as the skin does not expand with their growth. This process is called moulting.

- **Most caterpillars moult** four or five times before they enter the pupa or chrysalis stage.
- **In some species**, the caterpillars are armed with stinging hairs containing poisons. These hairs cause irritation or pain when touched.
- **Some male butterflies** have scent pockets on their wings, which disperse pheromones.
- **Butterflies do not have lungs** to breathe. They breathe through small holes in their abdomen, which are called spiracles.
- **Some butterflies migrate** in order to avoid bad weather, overcrowding, or to find a new place to live.

▼ *This caterpillar is protected from attack by predators, such as birds, by its irritating hairs.*

Butterfly features

- **Butterflies are** beautiful insects that belong to the order Lepidoptera. About 28,000 species of butterfly have been identified so far.
- **The earliest butterfly fossils** can be traced back to the Cretaceous Period, 130 million years ago.
- **Butterflies can live anywhere** in the world except in cold regions, such as Antarctica. They cannot withstand cold weather and have to maintain a body temperature above 30°C.
- **Like other insects**, butterflies have an exoskeleton, a hard outer covering that protects the body. A butterfly's body is also divided into three sections – head, thorax and abdomen. Butterflies have a pair of compound eyes.
- **The average lifespan of butterflies** is 20 to 40 days but some species can survive up to 10 months while others last only three to four days.

▲ *Butterflies, such as this small postman butterfly, usually hold their wings upright when they rest. Moths usually spread their wings out or fold them flat.*

  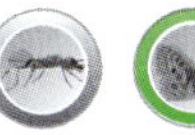   

- **Butterflies only consume** liquid food, such as flower nectar and liquids from rotten fruits or vines. Some feed on liquid animal waste.
- **Butterflies protect themselves** from predators, such as birds, lizards, bats and spiders, by mimicry and camouflage.
- **After bees**, butterflies are the second largest pollinators of crops.
- **Some butterflies** can be destructive too. Cabbage white butterflies feed on cabbages and can destroy entire crops.

...FASCINATING FACT...

Male butterflies attract the females by dancing around them. This is called a 'courtship dance'. While dancing, males secrete pheromones, a chemical scent that stimulates mating.

Tortoiseshell butterfly

- **Tortoiseshell butterflies** are large and brightly coloured butterflies found all over the world. They are one of the most common garden butterflies found in the UK.
- **Tortoiseshell butterflies** can also be found in the dense hill forests of Asia and northern USA.
- **Adult tortoiseshell butterflies** feed on fruit juices or the nectar from flowers, such as daisy and aster.
- **Female tortoiseshell butterflies** are larger than the male butterflies.
- **After mating**, a female tortoiseshell butterfly lays her eggs in batches on young nettle leaves. Each batch contains 60 to 100 eggs.
- **The eggs** hatch after about 10 days and the caterpillars spin a web over the nettle's growing tip. Tortoiseshell caterpillars live in groups and feed on the nettle leaves.
- **Tortoiseshell caterpillars** grow to about 2 cm in length within four weeks. They are black, with two yellow broken lines along their sides and are poisonous.

...FASCINATING FACT...

Tortoiseshell butterflies hibernate during the winter. Adults often hibernate in houses and sheds and can be spotted in the open between March and October, while caterpillars are seen between May to August.

- **Tortoiseshell butterfly** pupae are greyish brown and have metallic spots. These pupae are often seen hanging from posts, walls and tree trunks.
- **Tortoiseshell butterflies** used to be known as the 'devil's butterfly' in Scotland.

▲ *Adult tortoiseshell butterflies have a long life as adults, surviving for about 10 months from one summer to another.*

Red admiral butterfly

- **The red admiral butterfly** is easy to recognize. It is black in colour, with red bands and white markings on the upper and lower wings. Its wingspan is 4.5 to 7.6 cm.
- **Red Admirals are easily found** in gardens, orchards and woodlands across Europe, North America and Asia.

▼ *The name of the red admiral butterfly comes from its bright or 'admirable' colours.*

- **Adult red admiral butterflies** feed on flowers and rotting fruits, while caterpillars feed on nettle plants.
- **This species** is known for its migratory behaviour. Red admiral butterflies cannot survive cold winters. Once the winter sets in, they migrate to warmer places.
- **The red admiral** has a very erratic, rapid flight. Unusually for a butterfly, it sometimes flies at night.
- **Female red admiral** butterflies lay their eggs on nettle leaves. After seven days, the caterpillar emerges and folds leaves around itself to make a protective tent. The leaves are held together with silk threads and the caterpillar feeds inside its leaf shelter.
- **The caterpillars** are black to greenish-grey in colour and have a yellow line running along each side.
- **Adult red admiral butterflies** may hibernate in winter, storing enough fat in their bodies for survival.
- **Red admiral butterflies feed** on tree sap, rotting fruit and bird droppings. They also feed on the nectar of plants, such as common milkweed, red clover, aster and alfalfa.

FASCINATING FACT

Red admiral butterflies prefer moist woods, gardens, parks, marshes and moist fields. During migration, these butterflies can be found in almost any habitat, from the tundra in Canada to subtropical countries near the Equator.

Monarch butterfly

- **Monarch butterflies are found** all over the world, except in the cold regions. They are bright black and orange in colour and have a wingspan ranging up to 10 cm.

▲ *Canadians call this butterfly 'King Billy' because its orange and black colours are the same as those of King William of Orange, who was king of Great Britain from 1689–1702.*

- **Monarch butterflies use** their body colour to frighten off their enemies. The orange colour is considered a warning sign. They can also blend easily with the surroundings.
- **Monarch caterpillars** feed on milkweed plants, retaining the sap in their bodies even when they mature into butterflies. Birds attempting to eat monarchs dislike the taste and spit them out.
- **Monarchs are beneficial** for crops as they eat milkweed plants, which are weeds.
- **Monarch caterpillars** are brightly coloured, with bold black and white stripes. They are voracious eaters.
- **Male monarch butterflies** have dark spots called scent scales on their hind wings. Females do not have scent scales.

- **A monarch butterfly** takes approximately one month to mature from an egg into an adult butterfly. Adult monarch butterflies feed on flower nectar and water.
- **They are long distance migratory** insects and can migrate over 3200 km. Monarch butterflies guide themselves during migration using the position of the Sun and the magnetic field of the Earth.
- **Habitat destruction** and changes caused by logging are constant threats to monarch butterflies. Spraying of pesticides for weed control kills milkweed plants. This endangers the habitat and food source for these butterflies.

...FASCINATING FACT...

Monarch butterflies from northern USA and Canada migrate to the Sierra Madre Mountains, west of Mexico City, Mexico in the winter. The location was first discovered in 1975.

▶ *The white spots on the head and thorax of monarch butterflies act as an extra warning signal, which emphasizes to birds and reptiles that this butterfly tastes horrible.*

Bhutan glory butterfly

- **Bhutan glory butterflies** are found in Bhutan and north-eastern parts of Asia.
- **These butterflies** prefer to live in grass fields and undisturbed forests.
- **The wings** of Bhutan glory butterflies measure about 9 to 11 cm. They are black in colour.
- **Bhutan glory butterflies breed** twice a year from May to June and then August to October.
- **Very little** is known about the life history of Bhutan glory butterflies.
- **Experts believe** that these insects probably feed on the poisonous Indian birthwort plant.
- **Bhutan glory butterflies** protect themselves from predators by absorbing poison from the plants they feed on.
- **These butterflies** fly at altitudes of 1700–3000 m in the mountains.
- **Bhutan glory butterflies** were collected in large numbers in the past. Now, their numbers have been greatly reduced and they are very rare to spot.
- **Bhutan glory butterflies** are now listed as an endangered and protected species.

▶ *At rest, the Bhutan glory butterfly hides its colourful back wings with its front wings so it is well camouflaged. If disturbed, this butterfly quickly opens and shuts it wings, exposing its bright orange markings. These sudden flashes of colour may confuse a predator and allow the butterfly time to escape.*

Painted lady butterfly

- **The painted lady butterfly is popularly** known as the thistle butterfly because its caterpillar primarily feeds on thistle plants. It is also known as cosmopolite because it is found worldwide.
- **The painted lady** is one of the best-known butterflies in the world.
- **Painted lady butterflies** are mostly found in temperate regions across Asia, Europe and North America, especially around flowery meadows and fields.
- **These butterflies are primarily** black, brown and orange in colour. They have a wingspan of 4 to 5 cm.
- **Female painted lady butterflies** lay eggs on plants, such as thistles. After three to five days, they hatch into caterpillars. The caterpillars transform into pupae and finally emerge as colourful adult butterflies.
- **The caterpillar**, or larva, lives in a silky nest woven around the plant on which it feeds.
- **Adult painted lady butterflies** feed on nectar from flowers, such as aster, cosmos, ironweed and joe-pye weed.
- **An adult** painted lady butterfly lives for only two weeks.

...FASCINATING FACT...

Painted lady butterflies do not survive in winter. They die in the cold weather.

- **Painted lady butterflies are strong fliers** and long distance migrants. They can travel thousands of kilometres, sometimes with thousands of individuals flying together.

▼ *The painted lady butterfly can be distinguished from the tortoiseshell butterfly by the white marks on the black tips of its front wings.*

Birdwing butterfly

- **Female Queen Alexandra's birdwing** butterflies are the world's largest butterflies. They can grow up to 8 cm in length.
- **Birdwing butterflies** belong to the swallowtail group of butterflies. The butterflies have tails on their hind wings, like the wings of a swallow.
- **Male birdwing butterflies** are brightly coloured with yellow, pale blue and green markings.
- **Female birdwing butterflies** have cream and chocolate brown marking on their wings.
- **Predators avoid birdwing butterflies** because they are poisonous and distasteful. Birdwing caterpillars feed on the pipevine plants and absorb poisons from these plants.
- **A birdwing butterfly** lives for about seven months.
- **The birdwing butterfly** is listed as an endangered species. People are not allowed to hunt this insect.
- **The golden birdwing** and southern birdwing are some of the cousins of the Queen Alexandra's birdwing butterfly.
- **Birdwing butterflies are found** in tropical areas. The best time to spot these butterflies is in the early morning when they collect nectar from flowers.

...FASCINATING FACT...
Queen Alexandra's birdwing butterflies were named in honour of the wife of King Edward VII of England.

▲ *The beautiful Rajah Brooke's birdwing soars high in the rainforest canopy from Malaysia through to Sumatra and Borneo. It was named after the British Rajah Brooke of Sarawak by the famous naturalist Alfred Russell Wallace.*

Apollo butterfly

- **Apollo butterflies are mostly found** in mountains and hilly regions of Spain, central Europe, southern Scandinavia and Asia. Some Apollo butterflies live above an altitude of 4000 m and rarely descend to lower levels.
- **Apollo butterflies are cream in colour** with red and yellow eyespots on their wings. They are frail-looking butterflies but survive harsh weather conditions.

▲ *This mountain butterfly has a wingspan of 50 to 100 mm and a furry body to protect it from the cold. It survives the winter as a tiny caterpillar inside its egg.*

- **Habitat destruction** has made Apollo butterflies extremely rare. They are now an endangered species, protected by law in many countries.
- **The breeding season** of Apollo butterflies lasts from July to August. The female lays hundreds of eggs.
- **Female butterflies** lay round, white eggs either singly or in groups. The eggs usually hatch in the months of August and September.
- **Apollo caterpillars** feed on stonecrop plants.
- **These caterpillars moult** five times in their lifetime.
- **An adult Apollo butterfly** has a lifespan of a week.
- **Attempts are being made** to save Apollo butterfly populations by means of habitat management measures, reduction of insecticide use and observation of their behaviour during the time they are on the wing.

...FASCINATING FACT...

Adult butterflies use their proboscis, a kind of sucking tube, to feed on nectar from flowers, such as the thistle.

Peacock butterfly

- **Peacock butterflies** are named after their large, multi-coloured eyespots, which look like the 'eyes' on a real peacock's feathers. Adult peacock butterflies are light to dark brown in colour and have purplish-black lines.
- **These butterflies inhabit** the temperate regions of Europe and Asia. They are very commonly found in lowland England and Wales.

▼ *Peacock butterflies use the false eyes on their wings to scare predators away. They also open and close their wings rapidly to make a scraping sound as predators approach.*

- **Adult peacock butterflies** love to be around orchards, gardens and other places that have lots of flowers. They feed on the flower nectar of thistles, lavender and buddleia and also suck juices from overripe fruits.
- **Peacock caterpillars feed** on nettle plants. They live in groups.
- **Peacock butterflies have** a single brood in a year. Adults hibernate through the winter and emerge in the spring. They die after laying eggs, while the caterpillars hatch out and hibernate as adults.
- **Female peacock butterflies** can lay up to 500 eggs. The caterpillars emerge after one to two weeks and all live together in a communal web.
- **Fully grown caterpillars** are about 4 cm long. They have black-and-white spots and long black dorsal spines.
- **The pupae** are greyish-brown or greenish, with metallic gold spots.
- **The lifespan** of a peacock butterfly is relatively long and can even last up to one year.

... FASCINATING FACT ...

Peacock butterflies hibernate to avoid harsh winters. They take refuge in places such as hollow trees, rock crevices or stone walls. If disturbed, they create a hissing sound by rubbing their wings together.

Viceroy butterfly

▲ *The viceroy has a faster wingbeat than the monarch butterfly and also glides with its wings held horizontally, not held at an angle like the monarch.*

- **Viceroy butterflies** are mostly found in the USA, southern Canada and northern Mexico.
- **They have** black and orange patterns and white spots on their wings. These brilliant patterns make viceroy butterflies resemble monarch butterflies.

- **These butterflies are found** in meadows, marshes and swamps and other wet areas with trees, such as willow, aspen and poplar.
- **There are usually** two or three generations of viceroy butterflies born in each breeding season.
- **Viceroy butterflies** are known to mate in the afternoon. The female butterfly lays her eggs on the tips of poplar and willow leaves.
- **These eggs** hatch and the viceroy caterpillars feed on the leaves of trees such as willow and poplar. They are voracious eaters and even eat their own shells.
- **The caterpillars** are white and olive brown.
- **Adult viceroy butterflies feed** on the liquids from decaying fungi, dung and other animal waste.
- **Predators** often mistake viceroy butterflies for monarch butterflies, and avoid eating them. Viceroy butterflies are not poisonous.

...FASCINATING FACT...

Butterflies practice two kinds of mimicry – Batesian and Mullerian. In Batesian mimicry, a harmless species of butterfly mimics a toxic species. In Mullerian mimicry, two equally toxic species mimic each other for mutual benefit. Viceroy and monarch butterflies exhibit Batesian mimicry.

Moths

▲ *The Polyphemus moth has striking eyespots on its back wings and is named after Polyphemus, the one-eyed giant of Greek myths. It has a large wingspan of 90 to 140 mm and lives east of the Rocky Mountains from Canada down to Mexico.*

- **Moths make up about 90 percent** of the insects that belong to order Lepidoptera, which also includes butterflies. Insects that belong to this order have scaly wings.
- **Moths feed on nectar** as well as other plant and animal juices. Some moths do not feed as adults because they do not have mouthparts.

- **In some species of moth**, the females do not have wings.
- **Most moths are active** at night but there are some species of moth that remain active during the day.
- **Like butterflies**, some moths, such as hawk-moths, migrate long distances.
- **Some moths** have large spots on their wings. From a distance, these spots resemble the eyes of a fearsome animal and scare away potential predators.
- **Moths are masters** of mimicry and camouflage.
- **Some moths** can be mistaken for bird droppings when they lie still on the ground. This helps them escape to the eyes of predatory birds.
- **Species of moths** known as clothes moth are quite unusual. The larvae of these moths are destructive in nature and feed on different types of natural fabrics, such as wool, cotton, linen and even on fur, feathers and hair.

FASCINATING FACT

Tiger moths produce supersonic sound just like bats. These moths are known for their awful taste and bats avoid eating them.

Death's head hawk-moth

▶ *The caterpillars of Death's head hawk-moths reach 12.5 cm when fully grown and make a clicking sound if they are disturbed. They feed on potato plants and tomato leaves.*

- **Death's head hawk-moths** belong to the group of moths called sphinx moths. They are found in Africa, Asia and Europe.
- **This moth** is named after a peculiar mark, which is visible on its thorax. The mark looks like a ferocious skull.
- **Death's head hawk-moths** steal honey from bees' nests, which is why they are also known as 'bee robbers'.

...FASCINATING FACT...

The strange mark on the thorax of the death's head hawk-moth has given rise to many superstitions. In ancient times the presence of this moth was considered a sign of death.

  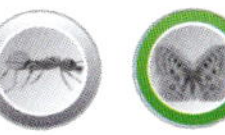   

- **At any point in its growth stage**, a death's head hawk-moth is capable of producing a loud squeaking sound to scare its predators away.
- **These moths** force air out of their strong, thick proboscis to make this squeaky sound.
- **Females** lay single eggs on different plants. They prefer to lay their eggs on potato and brinjal plants.
- **The caterpillars** have a horn on their tail end and are also known as hornworms.
- **To pupate**, the caterpillars make a mud cell deep in the soil and smoothe it by pushing their head against the wall of the cell.
- **Death's head hawk-moths** find it difficult to survive harsh winters and migrate to warmer places.

▶ *The skull pattern on the moth's thorax includes eye sockets and a jaw, while the yellow bands on its body look like ribs.*

Atlas moth

▼ *Giant Atlas moths have transparent triangles in the middle of each wing where the coloured scales are missing. These shiny patches may confuse predators by reflecting the light.*

FASCINATING FACT

Atlas moth cocoons hang from trees like fruits. These cocoons are used to produce a type of silk in Asia, known as Fagara silk.

- **Atlas moths** belong to the group of emperor moths and are known for their large size. These moths are named after the patterns on their wings, which look like maps.
- **Atlas moths are the largest moths**, with a wingspan of 24 to 30 cm. When they fly, these insects are often mistaken for birds.
- **Atlas moths are found** in tropical forests and are natives of south-east Asia.
- **The tips of their wings** are hooked and have patterns on them, which helps to scare predators away. These marks resemble the head of a snake.
- **Males** have large feathery antennae. These antennae are capable of sensing pheromones released by female atlas moths from a distance of several kilometres. Female pheromones attract males for mating.
- **Females** are much larger and heavier than the males. Their antennae are also less hairy.
- **Adults** do not have mouthparts so they cannot eat. They live for just two weeks and die soon after mating.
- **Females lay eggs** under leaves. These eggs hatch into greenish caterpillars, which feed on leaves.
- **Caterpillars** have fleshy projections all over their bodies. These caterpillars can grow up to 12 cm in length.

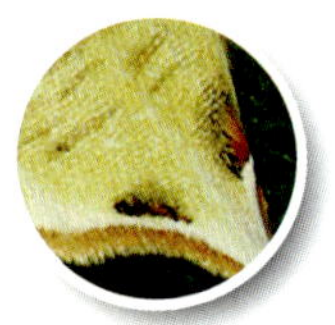

Swallowtail moth

- **Swallowtail moths** belong to the family geometridae of the order Lepidoptera.
- **Swallowtail moths are strikingly unusual moths** and can be mistaken for butterflies. They have slender bodies, thin legs and a short proboscis.
- **These moths are colourful** and sometimes fly in the day.
- **Swallowtail moths** are mainly found in tropical countries.
- **The brilliantly coloured species** are very large in size. Their colours are structural and do not contain pigments.
- **Some of the nocturnal species** have eyespots at the tip of their short pointed hind wings.
- **These eyespots** give an impression of a false head at the rear side of the moth, which protects it from predators. Therefore, during the day, these moths always rest on the upper side of leaves.
- **Not much is known** about the life history of swallowtail moths.
- **The size and marks** on the bodies differ in male and females.

...FASCINATING FACT...

Swallowtail moths derive their names from their resemblance to swallowtail butterflies. Their hindwings have a tail similar to that of swallowtail butterflies.

▲ *This large moth has broad wings, like a butterfly, but flies rapidly. In June and July, it is widespread and common in Europe and parts of Asia, often flying around lights.*

Hummingbird hawk-moth

▼ *The broad body of this robust little hawk-moth shows that it is a powerful flier. It holds its body still while hovering in front of flowers, beating its wings so fast that they are almost invisible. The rapidly beating wings produce a high-pitched hum, like the wings of a hummingbird.*

- **Hummingbird hawk-moths** belong to the hawk-moth group and are found all over the world.
- **Unlike other hawk-moths**, these moths fly during the day and can be easily spotted hovering over flowers in gardens and parks.
- **Hummingbird hawk-moths** are brownish in colour. They have black-and-white spots all over their body and their hind wings are orange.
- **These moths** have tufts of hair at the tip of their abdomen.
- **Like other butterflies and moths**, hummingbird hawk-moths have long, tubelike mouthparts that are coiled and tucked under their head.
- **These moths** use their long tongue to collect nectar from flowers.
- **The caterpillar** is slender and colourful. It has a horned tail, which gives it a fearsome look.
- **The moth pupates** in leaf litter (dead leaves, bits of bark, and other dead plant matter lying on the ground) and weaves a very thick cocoon.
- **People often mistake** this moth for a hummingbird because it hovers over flowers and sucks nectar from them, like a hummingbird.
- **Hummingbird hawk-moths** hibernate in winter to survive the cold weather.

Lobster moth

- **Lobster moths belong** to the group of moths known as prominent moths.
- **These moths** are commonly found in deciduous forests in Europe and Asia.
- **The wingspan** of lobster moths is about 5.5 to 7 cm.
- **Males** are often attracted towards the light. However, females are not fascinated by light.
- **The moth** appears in two colour forms – one with light front wings and one with dark front wings.
- **Lobster moths move** in a way that resembles the movements of ants.
- **The unusual shape** of lobster moth caterpillars often confuses their predators and scares them away.
- **As an act of defence**, the caterpillar curls back its large head and raises its legs in the air to startle small birds.
- **The caterpillar** constructs a silken cocoon and pupates in it.

...FASCINATING FACT...

Lobster moths are so-called as their larvae have six wiry, elongated legs and a swollen tale like a lobster.

▲ *A lobster moth caterpillar confuses predators by suddenly changing shape. It raises its head and tail over its body (making it look like a tiny lobster) and waves a pair of filaments at the end of its abdomen. Lobster moth caterpillars can also squirt formic acid over their predators.*

Peppered moth

- **Peppered moths** belong to a group of moths known as geometrid moths.
- **These moths** are delicate insects and have long legs and a slender body.
- **Peppered moth caterpillars** do not have any legs in the middle of their body. They hold onto branches with their first two pairs of specialized limbs called prolegs and a clasper at their tail end.
- **The antennae of male peppered moths** are feathery, while females have hair like antennae. The antennae of male peppered moths are also longer than those of females.
- **Males** are smaller and more slender in comparison with the larger and heavier female peppered moths.
- **Peppered moths are nocturnal** and usually rest on barks of lichen-covered trees during the day.
- **Peppered moth caterpillars** camouflage themselves by resembling a twig.
- **There are two varieties** of peppererd moths; a paler coloured variety, speckled with salt and pepper (black-and-white) marks while the other is coal-black in colour.

◀ *The pale coloured form of the peppered moth shows up better against dark backgrounds, making it more likely to be spotted by birds and other predators.*

◀ *The dark-coloured form of the peppered moth is less common today in industrial areas where pollution controls have cleaned up the air. The dark colour does not provide effective camouflage against clean tree trunks, which are often covered by pale-coloured lichens.*

- **During the Industrial Revolution**, the barks of many trees became blackish-grey in colour due to air pollution. Dark-coloured peppered moths blended with this polluted environment and matched the colour of the tree bark. Paler coloured peppered moths stood out as easy targets for birds and other hungry predators so more dark-coloured moths survived.

FASCINATING FACT

Peppered moth caterpillars are known as inchworms because they move their bodies in a looping fashion as though they are measuring the earth.

Moon moth

- **Moon moths belong to** the group known as Emperor moths. They are found all over the world, but are mostly seen in tropical countries.
- **Moon moths** have a white body and maroon legs. Their wings are bright green in colour. The colour of female moon moths is brighter than that of the males.
- **Moon moths have a wingspan** of about 10 to 13 cm and their tail is almost 8 cm long.

▼ *The eyespots on the wings of moon moths probably help to divert the attention of predators away from the moth's delicate body.*

- **The hind wings** of males are longer than those of the females. In overall size, male moon moths are much smaller than females.
- **Adult moon moths** have no mouthparts and do not eat anything. They do not live for more than a week.
- **Moon moths** make their cocoons in leaves. The silk of the cocoon does not shine and is brown in colour. This silk is not used commercially.
- **An adult female** lays about 250 eggs at a time, on walnut leaves. The eggs resemble seeds with grey specks on them.
- **Moon moths grow** only at the larval stage. If the larva grows into a small sized moth, the moth does not grow further in size.
- **Moon moth caterpillars** are bright apple green in colour and are beautifully segmented, with some white hairs.

... FASCINATING FACT ...

Moon moths are also called 'lunar moths' because of marks on their wings that look like a new moon.

Vinegar fly

▼ *Adult vinegar flies live for just two weeks, feeding on nectar and other sugary solutions. They survive longer as adults when the female has a choice of mates than when only one mate is available.*

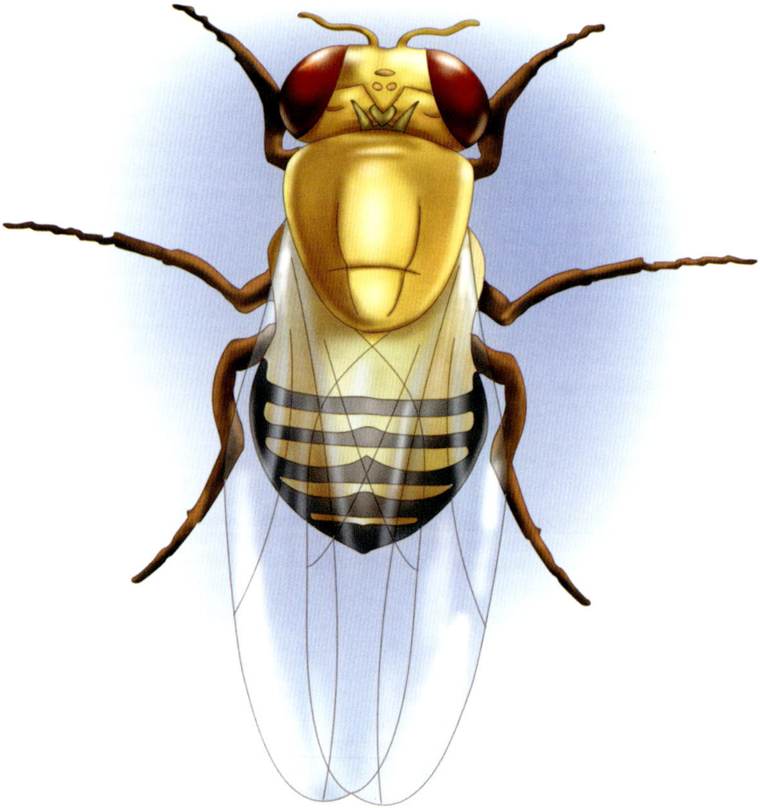

- **Vinegar flies** are tiny insects and measure about 2 mm in length.
- **Vinegar flies are also called pomace flies** because they are attracted by the sour smell of pomace, which is the liquid squeezed from fruit or seeds.
- **These insects** have large red eyes and their bodies are brownish yellow in colour.
- **Vinegar flies are not strong fliers** and can cover only short distances but these lightweight insects are easily carried along by the wind.
- **A female vinegar fly** can lay around 200 eggs if conditions are suitable.
- **The eggs** laid by female vinegar flies are not easily visible to the human eye. These eggs are normally found near decaying and fermented fruits and vegetables.
- **The larvae feed** on fermented food materials. They pupate and develop into adult flies in four to five days.
- **Several generations** can be produced in a couple of weeks, which is why these insects are suitable for scientific studies.
- **Vinegar flies** are used extensively for genetic research because their cells are strikingly similar to those of humans. Around 60 percent of their genes match with those of humans.
- **Vinegar flies** are considered pests because they can transmit germs and diseases from decaying food materials.

Horse fly

- **Horse flies** are strong-bodied flies with colourful patterns on their bodies.
- **Horse flies suck and feed** on the blood of humans and animals. These insects get their names, such as deer flies or moose flies, depending on the animal they feed on.

▼ *Horse flies are among the fastest flying insects, reaching maximum speeds of 39 km/h. Unlike most other flies, their flight can be silent, allowing females to sneak up on their prey.*

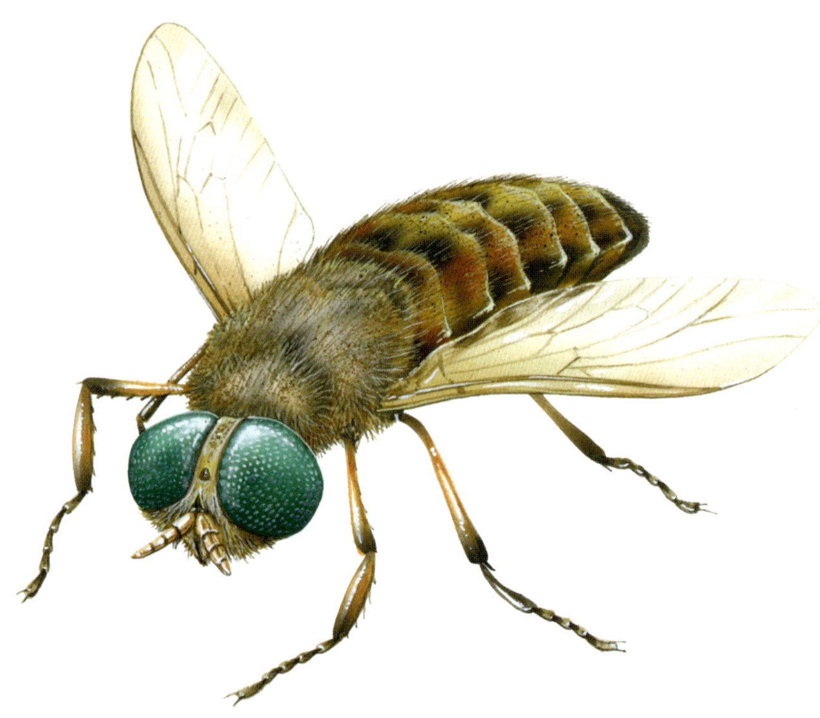

  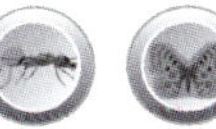   

- **There are about 25,000 species** of horse fly in the world.
- **Horse flies** have compound eyes, which are very prominent and occupy the entire surface of head in the males.
- **Colourful patterns** on the compound eyes are caused by the refraction of light. There are no pigments present in the eyes and as a result, the colour is not retained when these insects die.
- **The mouthparts** of these insects consist of a short powerful, piercing organ capable of penetrating tough skin. If undisturbed, horse flies can suck blood from their host for as long as half an hour.
- **Female horse flies** bite other animals to suck blood before they reproduce. However, male horse flies do not bite. They feed mainly on flower nectar and plant sap.
- **After mating**, females lay their eggs on plant and rock edges near water. The eggs are creamy white in colour.
- **Horse fly larvae feed** on soft-bodied insects and other small animals. They can become cannibalistic if there is a lack of food.
- **While biting** and sucking blood from animals, horse flies can transmit diseases such as anthrax.

Crane fly

- **Crane flies** belong to order Diptera and are closely related to mosquitoes.
- **These** long-legged insects are also known as 'daddy long legs'. Their legs are weakly attached to their body and often break off.
- **Some of the larger species** of crane fly, such as phantom craneflies, have legs that are as long as 2.5 cm.
- **Crane flies** have extremely narrow wings. They have a thin body and long legs and resemble large mosquitoes. These insects cannot bite.
- **Crane flies are nocturnal insects** and remain inactive in the day.
- **Females** lay their eggs in moist soil. The eggs hatch into larvae, which are greyish to pale brown in colour.
- **The larvae** of crane flies feed on dead and decaying matter. Some species also feed on other small insects and others eat plant roots.
- **Crane fly larvae** are also known as leatherjackets because of their tough, brown skin. They are often used as fishing bait.
- **Farmers dislike** the larvae of these insects because they damage the roots and turf of grain fields and grass crops.
- **A rare species** of crane fly does not have wings. These insects are found in Hawaii.

▲ *The very long, thin legs of a crane fly are usually twice as long as its body. Apart from their long legs, crane flies can be recognized by the V-shaped groove on the top of their thorax.*

House-fly

- **House-flies** belong to the order Diptera and are one of the most common insects.
- **Like all flies**, house-flies have small projections below their front wings known as halteres, which help them to fly. Halteres are modified hind wings, which are used for landing and balancing.
- **House-flies feed** on liquid food and do not bite animals and other insects. The mouthparts of a house-fly are like a sponge, which absorbs liquid food.
- **House-flies often vomit** some portion of their last feed on top of new food particles. This makes the new food material easier to digest.
- **Most of the time**, house-flies do not eat all the food and leave some particles behind. These remaining food particles can spread a variety of diseases.
- **House-flies** are considered to be the most dangerous vector. A vector is an organism, such as a mosquito or tick, which carries disease-causing micro-organisms from one host to another.
- **House-flies** have compound eyes and 4000 individual lenses form each eye. These insects cannot see the colour red.

...**FASCINATING FACT**...

House-flies are known to spread forty serious diseases. A single fly harbours as many as 33,000,000 infectious organisms inside its intestines and 500,000,000 on its body surface and legs.

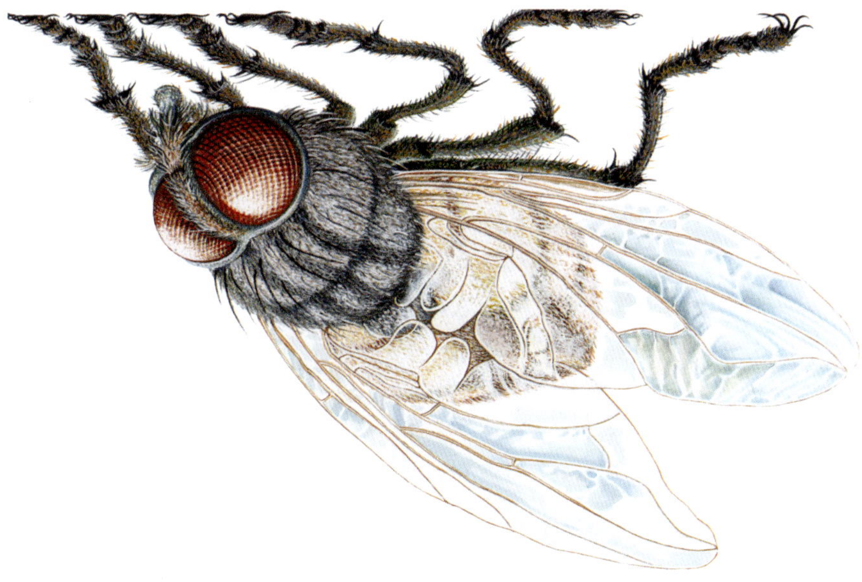

▲ *Sticky pads and sharp claws enable house-flies to walk upside down with ease. Fine hairs on the tip of a house fly's legs also enable it to 'taste' liquids.*

- **Female house-flies** can lay more than 600 to 1000 eggs in a lifetime. However, most offspring do not survive to reproduce.
- **Common house-flies** are normally found wherever there is human activity. They thrive on the waste materials left behind by humans and other animals.

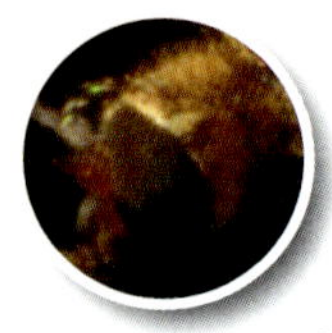

Mosquito

- **Mosquitoes** are the only flies of the order Diptera that have scaly wings.
- **Most female mosquitoes** have to feed on the blood of other animals to reproduce. They need the protein extracted from blood for the development of their eggs.
- **The eggs** float on water and hatch to produce aquatic larvae known as wrigglers.
- **The larvae** cannot breathe underwater and 'hang' from the water's surface to take in air.
- **Mosquito larvae** pupate in the water itself. The pupa is not completely immobile. It can change position according to the light and wind conditions in its environment.
- **Adult male mosquitoes** feed on nectar and other plant fluids. Only female mosquitoes feed on blood.
- **Male mosquitoes** cannot bite. Their mouthparts are modified for sucking only.
- **Mosquitoes** have infrared vision. They can sense the warmth of other insects and animals.

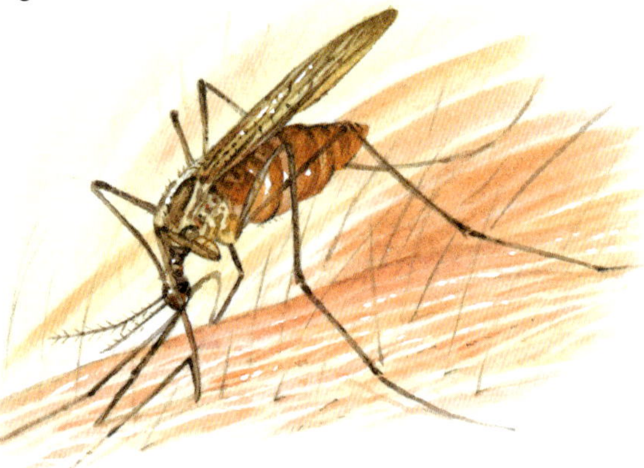

▲ *A female mosquito uses her needle-like mouthparts to pierce a victim's skin and suck up a blood meal. She injects a salivary fluid to keep the blood flowing and stop it from the clotting.*

- **Dragonflies feed** on mosquitoes and are also known as mosquito hawks. Dragonfly nymphs also feed on mosquito larvae.
- **Mosquitoes are known** to spread many infectious diseases, such as yellow fever and dengue fever. The female Anopheles mosquito spreads malaria.

▼ *The female mosquito's long, sharp proboscis is longer than her antennae. She has few hairs on her antennae but the male mosquito has very feathery antennae to pick up the female's scent.*

Firefly

▲ *A female firefly signals to a mate with her glowing tail.*

- **Fireflies** are not flies but a type of beetle. These insects are also known as lightning bugs.
- **Fireflies can grow** up to 2.5 cm in length and live for three to four months. Female fireflies live longer than the males.
- **Fireflies** have a special organ under their belly, which emits flashes of green or yellow light.
- **The light** is known as 'cold light'. This process of producing light is also known as bioluminescence. No other insects except fireflies can produce light from their own bodies.

- **Fireflies emit** only light energy. A normal light bulb emits only 10 percent of the energy as light. The remaining 90 percent is emitted as heat energy. Fireflies do not emit any heat energy.
- **Male and female fireflies** emit light to attract mates.
- **Fireflies are nocturnal** in nature. They live on plants and trees during the day and are active at night.

▲ *Each species of firefly has its own unique sequence of flashes to attract a mate of the same species. Some male fireflies flash in synchrony, which may help them to attract females more easily.*

FASCINATING FACT

Some female fireflies fool males of other species by flickering their light. When the males come closer to mate, the females eat them up.

- **Female fireflies** and their larvae are carnivorous and feed on snails, slugs and other worms. Most male fireflies don't eat but some may feed on pollen and nectar.
- **Some female fireflies are wingless** and are also known as glow-worms.

Goliath beetle

- **The Goliath beetle** is one of the largest and heaviest insects in the world. Males are as heavy as an apple.
- **Goliath beetles grow** up to 12 cm and weigh about 115 g.
- **Found** in many colours, most Goliath beetles have black and white spots on their wings.
- **Goliath beetles** used to be found only in Africa. Today, however, these insects can be found in almost all parts of the world.
- **Males** have a horn-shaped structure on their heads. They often fight each other with their horns.
- **Goliath beetles are good fliers**. They produce a low, helicopter-like whir while flying.
- **By feeding on** dead plant and animal tissues, Goliath beetles help to keep the environment clean.
- **A fossil** of the oldest goliath beetle dates is almost 300 million years old.
- **Scientists believe** that goliath beetles, like some other insects, were much larger in prehistoric times. This may because there was more oxygen in the air long ago.

...FASCINATING FACT...
The Goliath beetle is named after the Biblical giant, Goliath.

▲ *The male Goliath beetle would only just fit on your hand! Adult beetles cannot grow, which means that Goliath beetles also have giant larvae.*

Diving beetle

- **Diving beetles** have an oval body, which is brown or black in colour. Their wings are shiny and look metallic green when light reflects off their body. Diving beetles are commonly found in ponds and other still water.
- **A diving beetle** has strong hairy legs, which it uses like oars of a rowing boat to push its body forwards while swimming.
- **These insects** cannot breathe underwater and have to come to the water's surface to breathe air. They store this air under their wing covers.
- **Diving beetles often fly** at night in search of new ponds.
- **The beetles locate** new ponds with the help of the light that reflects from water surfaces. They often get confused with light that is reflected from a glass surface and mistake it for water.
- **The female diving beetle** is much bigger in size than the male beetle.
- **Females** make small slits in a plant stem and lay their eggs inside.
- **The larvae float** on the surface of the pond and move to the shore to pupate.
- **The larvae** are known as 'water tigers' because they can attack and bite other insects. They can even eat tadpoles and small fish.
- **Diving beetles feed** on other water insects, small fishes and tadpoles.

▼ *The great diving beetle has a flattened, streamlined body, which helps it to swim rapidly. It moves its back legs together, rather than alternately like most other water beetles. When the beetle stops swimming, it floats to the surface of the water.*

Bombardier beetle

- **Bombardier beetles** are ground beetles. They have a black body and their wings have bright yellow spots on them.
- **The wing covers** of bombardier beetles are fused together. These insects cannot fly but they are very fast runners.

▼ *The bombardier beetle can twist the end of its abdomen to squirt out a poisonous spray in almost any direction. The spray turns into a protective smoke screen, which gives the insect time to escape.*

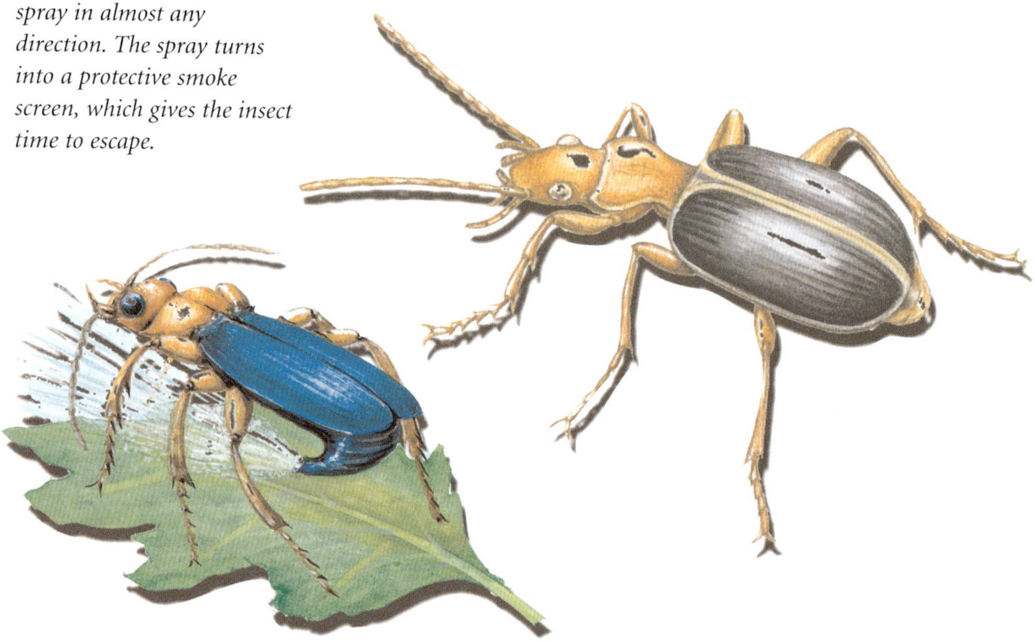

- **Bombardier beetles** have an interesting defence strategy and are often compared to mobile chemical laboratories.
- **Two separate chambers** within the beetle's body contain chemicals – hydrogen peroxide and hydroquinone. These chemicals fuse together in a 'fusion chamber' to form a noxious toxin, which causes irritation.
- **The temperature** of this toxic liquid is 100°C. It is squirted out from the beetle's body immediately, otherwise the bombardier beetle would explode from within.
- **Bombardier beetles** use a cannon-like body part to spray the liquid at their predators. It is situated on their abdomen.
- **The liquid evaporates** immediately after it is sprayed and forms a gas that temporarily blinds the enemy, while the bombardier beetle runs away.
- **Bombardier beetles spend** most of their time in rotting wood and lay eggs on plant remains and other decomposing matter.
- **These beetles** are scavengers and come out at night. Their larvae are carnivorous and feed on other insects.

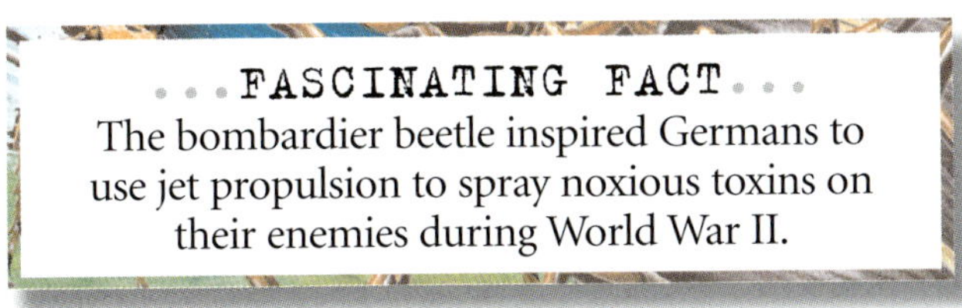

FASCINATING FACT

The bombardier beetle inspired Germans to use jet propulsion to spray noxious toxins on their enemies during World War II.

Tiger beetle

- **Tiger beetles** are usually shiny metallic colours, such as green, brown, black and purple. They often have stripes just like tigers.
- **The smallest tiger beetles** live in Borneo and measure up to 6 mm. The largest tiger beetles live in Africa and are as large as 44 mm.
- **Tiger beetles are found** in sunny, sandy areas and are active during the day. However, there are some species that come out at night.

- **Tiger beetles are good fliers** and fly in a zigzag pattern if a predator approaches them. They are also very fast runners.
- **These insects are predatory** in nature. Once they locate their prey, they pounce on it and use their jaws to tear it into pieces.
- **Tiger beetles** taste awful and their predators avoid eating them.
- **Female tiger beetles** lay their eggs in burrows in the ground. The burrow can be almost 0.5 m deep.
- **The larvae** of tiger beetles have a pair of powerful and large jaws, which are used to capture small insects.
- **Some species** of tiger beetles are endangered or nearing extinction. This is because of the lack of undisturbed sandy areas in which they can breed.

FASCINATING FACT

In Borneo, a type of locust mimics tiger beetles to save itself from its predators.

◀ *Tiger beetles have huge eyes with which to see their prey and massive biting jaws to catch and cut up their food.*

Stag beetle

- **Stag beetles** are usually brown or black in colour but there are some species that are bright green and red.
- **These beetles live** in damp wooded areas, especially near oak woodlands.
- **Stag beetles** have mandibles (jaws), which resemble the antlers of a stag.
- **Males** have long and ferocious looking jaws. The jaws of females are not as long as those of the males.
- **Males use** their antlers to attract females. They rarely use their jaws to fight or defend themselves.
- **At dusk** male stag beetles fly in search of females to mate. They fly in an irregular fashion and often get misguided by bright lights.
- **The larvae** of these insects feed on rotten wood and plant remains.
- **The larvae take a long time** to develop into mature adults because the food on which they feed is not nutritious.
- **Adult stag beetles** do not eat anything because they have enough reserve energy stored as fat. However, they do feed on the sweet sap of trees.

...FASCINATING FACT...

Stag beetles are also known as 'pinching bugs' because they can nip with their jaws and draw blood from human beings.

▲ *These lesser stag beetles have much smaller jaws than the larger the elephant or giant, stag beetle of North America. Stag beetles belong to the scarab beetle superfamily, which contains over 20,000 species.*

Rhinoceros beetle

- **Rhinoceros beetles** are believed to be the strongest creatures on Earth. They can carry about 850 times their own weight.
- **These beetles can grow** up to 13 cm in length.
- **The preferred habitat** of rhinoceros beetles is tropical rainforests where the vegetation is thick and there is plenty of moisture in the atmosphere.
- **Rhinoceros beetles** are named after the horns on their head, which resemble spikes.
- **Only males** have horns. The larger the horn, the better are their chances of winning a mate's attention.
- **The horns** are very strong and can pierce through the exoskeletons of insects.
- **Rhinoceros beetles do not use** their horns for defending themselves from predators. Instead, they use them to fight with other males for food and to attract female beetles for mating.
- **Rhinoceros beetles are nocturnal** in nature and almost all their hunting and feeding activities take place at night.
- **These beetles** help to keep the jungle clean and feed on plant sap and rotten fruits that have fallen on the ground.
- **Rhinoceros beetles are known** to be fierce fighters. Natives in some parts of Thailand hold beetle fighting competitions to watch these beetles fight.

▲ *This rhinoceros beetle has two horns, but some beetles have three, or even five, horns. The very tough exoskeleton protects the beetle's body like a suit of armour.*

Ladybird beetle

- **Ladybird beetles, or ladybugs,** were dedicated to the Virgin Mary. They were known as 'beetle of Our Lady' during the Medieval period.
- **Ladybirds** are almost circular in shape. They are bright pink, orange or red with black and red or orange spots. The number of spots may vary from species to species. Ladybirds are found in temperate and tropical regions all over the world.
- **These beetles** are one of the most beneficial insects because they feed on insect pests that damage crops.
- **Ladybirds** are sometimes bred on a large scale and are then introduced into farms or greenhouses to get rid of pests. However, some species of ladybirds are herbivorous and are considered pests themselves.
- **These insects are easily mistaken** for leaf beetles because of their similar colouring and spots.
- **When disturbed**, ladybirds secrete a foul smelling fluid, which causes a stain. This is called reflex-bleeding.
- **Both adults and larvae** eat aphids, scale insects and other soft-bodied insects.
- **Ladybird larvae** do not have wings. They are metallic blue in colour with bright yellow spots all over their body. Their bright colour warns birds not to eat them.
- **The halloween ladybird** is a pumpkin-orange coloured beetle found in the USA during late October. It is named after Halloween since it is often seen during this festival.
- **Adult ladybirds hibernate** in huge clusters in densely vegetated areas, usually at high altitudes.

▶ *The bright colours of adult ladybirds warn predators that they taste horrible and are best left alone. Hidden under the brightly coloured wing cases are two delicate flying wings.*

True bugs

- **True bugs** belong to the suborder Heteroptera of the order Hemiptera. There are at least 55,000 different kinds of bugs.
- **These bugs** generally have two pairs of wings. The first pair is partially hard and protects the delicate membrane-like second pair of wings.

▲ *The word 'bug' is sometimes used to mean any insect, but a true bug is an insect with piercing and sucking mouthparts, which are tucked beneath the head when not in use.*

- **Some bugs** do not have wings while the nymphs of all bugs are wingless.
- **True bugs have compound eyes** and their mouthparts are adapted for sucking and piercing. Most bugs have beaks that are segmented into four or five parts.

- **Bugs undergo incomplete metamorphosis**. There is no pupal stage and the bugs grow into adults by moulting again and again. The nymphs resemble the adult bugs.
- **Bugs can survive** on land, in air, on the surface of water and even under water. There are very few places where you would not find a bug.
- **Some bugs can give out** a very bad odour. This is a defence strategy .
- **Bugs feed** on plant and animal juices. There are some bugs, such as bed bugs, which are parasites. They live by sucking blood from other animals.
- **Carnivorous bugs** are predatory and help to control pests while herbivorous bugs are a threat to crops. Bugs can be cannibalistic and may feed on weaker individuals of their own kind.

...FASCINATING FACT...

Some people cultivate certain species of bugs to obtain dyes from them, while others relish bugs as food. Bugs are often harvested on a commercial scale for various purposes.

Assassin bug

▲ *An assassin bug may take several days to eat a large victim. Its front legs have powerful muscles for holding prey while sucking out their body fluids.*

- **Assassin bugs** are either black or brown or bright red and black in colour.
- **The wings** of assassin bugs lie flat on their abdomen. These insects have long legs, which are adapted for running.
- **Assassin bugs are predatory**. They grab their prey and 'assassinate' it by injecting venom. This venom is so powerful that caterpillars, which are several times larger than assassin bugs, can be killed in a few seconds.
- **The venom** paralyzes the prey and partially dissolves and disintegrates it. The bug then sucks the liquid food.
- **Assassin bugs** have a powerful curved beak, which is used for sucking the blood of other insects, larger animals and even humans.
- **Male and female assassin bugs** are similar in appearance but sometimes the females do not have wings.
- **Assassin bugs** give out a pungent smell, which, along with their poisonous bite, protects them from their predators.
- **An assassin bug's bite** can be quite painful and can transmit germs and diseases. These bugs are known to spread a disease called Chagas' disease.
- **A species of assassin bug**, known as the masked assassin bug, camouflages itself by sticking dirt to its body.

FASCINATING FACT

The saliva of assassin bugs can cause temporary blindness in humans.

Squash bug

- **Squash bugs are named** because they are a threat to squash and other related plants. These can usually be found in colours ranging from brown to black.
- **Some squash bugs** have leaflike extensions on their hind legs. This makes them look like dead leaves, which helps with camouflage. These bugs are called leaf-footed bugs.

- **With their powerful beaks**, squash bugs can easily pierce and suck fluids from plants and insects.
- **Squash bugs have scent glands** that emit a pungent smell. However, the odour is not as strong as that of stink bugs.
- **While most** squash bugs are carnivorous, a few feed on both plants and insects, and some are strictly vegetarian.
- **While feeding**, the squash bug injects a toxic substance into the plant. As a result, the plant wilts and dies.
- **Squash bugs lay their eggs** in clusters on plants. The eggs are oval, flattish or elongated in shape.
- **The nymphs** that hatch from these eggs resemble black ants and moult four to five times before maturing into adults.
- **Farmers consider** squash bugs to be dangerous pests and adopt various measures to get rid of them.

...FASCINATING FACT...
A rice field affected by squash bugs can be smelt from a considerable distance.

◀ *The squash bug of North America feeds on the juices of cucumber, squash, melon, pumpkin and other gourds. It does not have leaflike back legs.*

Cicada

- **Cicadas** belong to the order Homoptera and are related to true bugs.
- **Most species** of cicada are found in deserts, grasslands and forests.
- **Cicadas have** large and colourful wings. They hold their wings in a slanting position over their abdomen, like a tent.
- **Cicadas emit** a sound similar to that of a knife grinder, a railway whistle and even to fat spitting in an overheated pan.
- **Male cicadas** sing loudly to attract females, with the help of special drumlike membranes called timbals. Female cicadas do not produce any sound because their timbals are not developed.
- **Large swarms of cicadas** attract birds, which feast on these insects.

▼ *Cicadas have four pairs of membranous wings, although the front pair of wings are twice the length of the back pair. They suck plant juices with beaklike mouthparts located beneath the head.*

▶ *Cicada eggs hatch into wingless nymphs. Most cicadas spend between one and three years as nymphs, growing and moulting as they gradually develop into adults.*

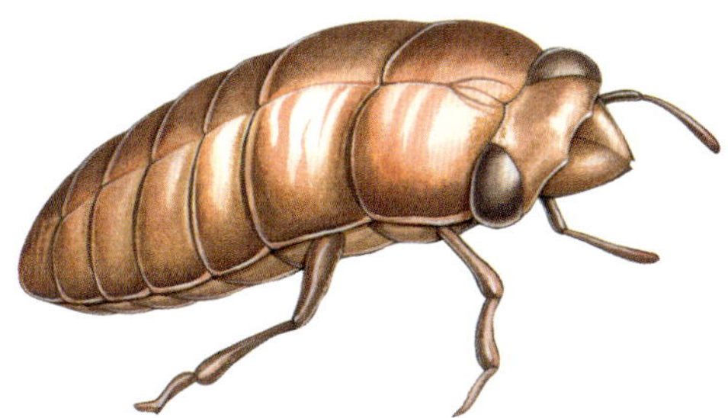

...FASCINATING FACT...
In Borneo, Malaysia and many other areas of the South Pacific, people eat cicadas.

- **Female cicadas** lay their eggs on plants and tree twigs. When the eggs hatch, the nymphs fall to the ground. The nymphs live underground for many years, feeding on the roots of plants. Later, they emerge from the ground, climb up trees and then moult.
- **Adult cicadas** do not live as long as the nymphs. They only survive a few weeks.
- **A species of cicada** known as the periodical cicada is found in America. It emerges from under the ground every 13 or 17 years. These insects are one of the longest-lived in the world.

Spittlebug

- **Spittlebug nymphs** are not easy to spot because they are often hidden in a frothy mass on leaves.
- **These bugs are named** after the spitlike frothy mass secreted by the nymphs. This froth is sometimes known as cuckoo-spit.
- **Cuckoo-spit** protects the spittlebug nymphs from predators.
- **The froth** also helps the nymphs to control their temperature and even prevents them from losing moisture and drying out.
- **Some spittlebug nymphs** form delicate tubes about 10 to 12 mm in length. They attach these tubes along the sides of twigs and live there after filling them with spittle.
- **Spittlebugs are considered** to be pests as they feed on the sap of plants.

▶ *Spittlebug nymphs produce 'cuckoo spit' by giving off a sticky liquid and blowing it into a frothy mass of white bubbles. As well as hiding the nymph from predators, these bubbles also protect the young bug from the drying effects of the sun.*

...FASCINATING FACT...

In Madagascar, spittlebugs discharge a clear liquid instead of foam, which falls to the ground like rain.

- **Spittlebugs** are found in different shades of yellow and brown. They have a triangular head, red eyes and spotted wings.
- **Spittlebugs** have a froglike appearance and are also known as froghoppers. They are good jumpers but they rarely fly, even though these insects have well-developed wings.
- **Adult spittlebugs** have rather large heads in comparison with their small bodies.

▲ *Adult spittlebugs do not produce foamy spittle like their nymphs. They spend their time hopping about like tiny frogs on the plants and shrubs from which they feed. The females lay their eggs in the stems of grasses and other plants.*

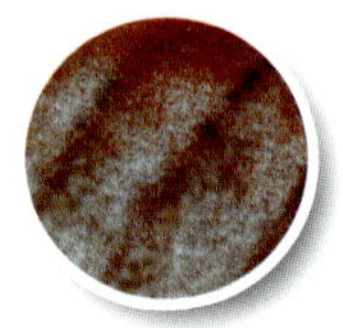

Mealybug

◀ *Mealybug nymphs do not usually move after their first moult. They stay in one place, joined to plants only by their sucking mouthparts.*

- **Mealybugs** are very small insects up to 3 mm long. They are found in huge clusters on leaves, twigs and tree bark. These bugs are also called coccids.
- **Females** do not usually have wings, eyes or legs and remain immobile on plants. They are always covered in a white sticky coating of their own secretion. This protective coating looks like cornmeal.
- **Males** do not have mouthparts. However, they have wings and can fly.
- **Female mealybugs** never lay their eggs in the open. The eggs are attached to their bodies. However, some species of mealybugs can give birth to live young.

- **The flat**, oval larvae crawl about quite actively at first, but soon lose their legs and cover themselves with their mealy secretions.
- **A male mealybug's** hind wings are modified into tiny structures called halteres.
- **Mealybugs feed** on the sap extracted from the plant tissues and are considered to be pests of citrus trees and greenhouse plants.
- **Mealybugs can** harm plants in many ways. Galls can form on plants, or their stems can become twisted and deformed.
- **Mealybugs produce** a sugary substance known as honeydew. Ants often visit these insects for this sweet-tasting secretion.
- **Beetles**, lacewings and caterpillars prey on mealybugs.

▲ *Male mealybugs, or scale insects, usually have only one pair of delicate wings, well-developed legs and antennae and no mouthparts. Females on the other hand are often wingless and legless, with reduced antennae. The females also secrete a mass of waxy threads as a protective covering (above).*

Aphid

- **Aphids** are related to cicadas. They can be found in green, red or brown colours and are also called greenfly.
- **They have** a large pear-shaped abdomen with two slender tubes called cornicles attached to it. The cornicles secrete wax.
- **Aphids** may or may not have wings. Those with wings are weak fliers, but they can cover great distances with the help of air currents.
- **Many aphids** live underground and suck sap from roots. Sometimes, these insects depend upon ants to carry them through tunnels in the soil and leave them out on fresh roots.

- **Aphids produce sugary honeydew.** This is because they cannot digest all the plant sugar they eat. The honeydew is clear and sweet but it becomes black because a fungus grows on it.
- **Many other insects**, especially ants, feed on the honeydew. In return, the ants protect the aphids from their predators, build shelters, 'graze' them in fresh pastures and even take them into their ant nests during bad weather.
- **Some aphids lay eggs** but some can reproduce without mating. These aphids give birth to live young by the process of parthenogenesis.
- **Aphids breed** in huge numbers. An aphid can produce up to 100 young at a time.
- **Some aphids** secrete long, curly strands of a waxlike substance from their cornicles. These aphids form dense colonies, which can be seen from many metres away.
- **Aphids** can cause damage to plants. Their saliva causes plant leaves to fold and curl and even form galls.

◀ *The cornicles are very obvious on the abdomens of these two aphids. The special waxy fluid produced from these tubes (bottom right) may help to protect the aphids from predators.*

Leafhopper

- **Leafhoppers** are a bug related to cicadas. They have a very distinct leaflike shape and colour and are easy to recognize.
- **Leafhoppers can survive** in almost any part of the world. They are terrestrial bugs and can be found in deserts as well as in marshy and moist places.
- **Strong fliers**, leafhoppers are also capable of jumping considerable distances.
- **If these insects** feed on plants, they can cause the leaves to curl and affect the plant's growth.
- **Leafhoppers** are considered pests and can cause damage to crops.
- **Leafhoppers search** for their mates by making special mating calls.
- **Females lay their eggs** in slits made in plant stems. The eggs can remain dormant for a month. In some species, the eggs can even remain dormant for a year.
- **Like aphids**, leafhoppers produce honeydew from the excess plant sap that they feed on.
- **These bugs** communicate with each other by producing low frequency sounds, which humans cannot hear.
- **Birds**, reptiles and large insects, such as wasps, are a threat to leafhoppers.

▶ *Leafhoppers are very common jumping insects that look rather like a narrow version of an adult spittlebug, or froghopper. They are tiny insects, which are only 2 to 15 mm long.*

Stinkbug

▲ *In some stinkbugs, the thorax extends down the back to form a protective shield, which almost covers the abdomen. These stinkbugs are also called shield bugs.*

- **Stinkbugs have glands** on their undersurface, from which they secrete a fluid. This fluid has a foul odour, which is why these insects are called stinkbugs.
- **Their scent** has a strong effect on many animals and protects the bug from predators.
- **Stinkbugs can be found** in many colours, such as green, grey, brown, red, black and yellow. They are one of the most notorious pests found in farmlands and orchards.
- **Some species** of stinkbugs produce a loud sound to defend themselves.

 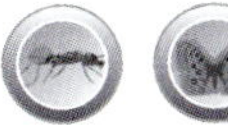   

- **Stinkbugs have a compound** called glycerol in their blood. This prevents their blood from freezing in winter.

...FASCINATING FACT...
In some parts of Mexico, India and Africa, stinkbugs are relished as a source of food.

- **Many species** of stinkbug are active during the day, while others are nocturnal, especially the dark-coloured species, which live in thick grass or under the leaves.
- **Stinkbugs normally feed** on the sap from flowers, leaves and fruits, which is why they destroy crops.
- **Male and female stinkbugs** are very similar in appearance even though the male is much smaller in size.
- **The young nymphs** do not have wings but the adult stinkbugs are very good at flying.

▶ *Stinkbugs range between 5 and 12 mm in length. They all have antennae made up of five segments.*

Water boatman

- **Water boatmen** are aquatic insects and are usually found in ponds and other freshwater bodies, such as canals and ditches.
- **Water boatmen** have powerful, hairy legs and are named after their habit of using their legs as oars 'row' themselves through the water.
- **Most species** of water boatman can fly. However, these insects usually cling to water plants or live at the bottom of ponds.
- **Water boatmen do not have gills** and have to come to the surface to breathe.
- **Hairs** on the body trap air bubbles. This helps water boatmen to stay under water for long periods.
- **Water boatmen feed** on algae, plants and decaying animal matter.
- **Some males** rub their legs together to make squeaky sounds that attract females.
- **The females** lays her eggs under water. The young nymphs that hatch from the eggs resemble adult water boatmen (without wings) but they moult five times before they become winged adults.

...FASCINATING FACT...

People in Mexico dry water boatmen eggs and eat them. In some countries, water boatmen are also sold as bird food.

▼ *Water boatmen are not buoyant enough to float, so when they stop swimming, they sink to the bottom. This is useful because they feed on the bottom of ponds, canals and ditches, using their shovel-like front legs to scrabble up food.*

Backswimmer

- **Backswimmers** spend almost their entire life floating in an upsidedown position in ponds. They use their legs like oars and resemble rowing boats.
- **While floating**, backswimmers identify direction with the help of light.
- **Unlike other insects**, the underside of backswimmers is dark in colour while the top of the body is light. The dark colour helps to hide the backswimmer from predators.

- **Backswimmers** come to the water surface for air. They carry a bubble of air under their belly, which helps them to stay underwater for a long time. This air bubble makes them look silvery in appearance.
- **These insects** fly from one pond to another in search of food.
- **Backswimmers feed** on other water insects, worms and tadpoles.
- **Also known** as the water bees, the backswimmer's bite is painful. It can even bite humans.
- **In appearance**, backswimmers look very similar to water boatmen. However, water boatmen float the right way up and feed mainly on plants. Backswimmers, in contrast, are predators.
- **When attacking**, backswimmers inject toxins into their prey. This has a chemical reaction, which kills the prey.
- **Some species** of backswimmers are known to hibernate. During winter, these insects are found moving under the surface of frozen water.

◀ *Backswimmers are shaped like boats, with a prominent keel along their back. As the bug swims on its back, the keel points downwards, like the keel on a real boat. The reservoir of air held beneath the body makes the insect float to the surface if it stops swimming. Claws on the end of each leg help the bug to hang upside down from the surface of the water or grip onto water plants.*

Giant water bug

▲ *Giant water bugs store air in a dip between the roof of the abdomen and the wings. To renew this air supply, they back up to the surface of the water and extend a snorkel-like tube above the surface.*

- **Giant water bugs** are like snorkellers. They have flaplike back legs to help them swim fast and special breathing tubes that resemble a snorkel.
- **By lying still** in the water giant water bugs camouflage themselves so that they look like dead leaves.

FASCINATING FACT

Female giant water bugs lay their eggs on the backs of the males. They secrete a waterproof glue to stick the eggs onto the male's back.

- **These insects can fly** but they can survive for only about 15 minutes if they are taken out of water.
- **Giant water bugs** are fierce predators that feed on tadpoles, fish and other insects.
- **Giant water bugs hold their prey** with their claws and inject venom to paralyze it. Their mouthparts help them to pierce and suck fluid.
- **Giant water bugs help to control** the mosquito population by feeding on mosquito larvae.
- **Males carry fertilized eggs** on their backs for about 10 days. They take good care of the eggs and prevent fungus from growing on them until they hatch.
- **Giant water bugs** are also known as 'toe biters' because they may bite humans on the toes while they are wading in the water.
- **In some** Asian countries, giant water bugs are considered a tasty snack.

Water strider

- **Water striders are** often found floating on still water and slow moving streams. They are one of the few insects that can survive in the sea and have even been found floating on the surface of the Pacific Ocean.
- **Water striders** seldom go underwater. Their long legs help them to skate and steer across the water. They are also called pond skaters.
- **These insects have six legs**, although it seems as if they have only four. The front two legs are short and are used mainly to grasp the prey. The hind legs are very long and can be twice the length of the body.
- **Water striders have** long, slender and hairy legs, which end in a pad of water repellent hairs so they do not break through the surface of the water.
- **Some adults** have wings, while others are wingless.
- **Water striders feed** on insects that fall into the water and aquatic insects that come to the surface to breathe.
- **Water striders communicate** with each other by making vibrations and ripples on the water's surface.
- **Water striders move very quickly** and can run across water. If they were as big as humans, they would move as fast as a jet plane.
- **Adults** hibernate throughout winter and mate in the spring.

▶ *The long, thin legs of a water strider help to spread out its weight. The surface of the water bends into small dips around the end of each leg, but does not break.*

...FASCINATING FACT...

Water striders are also known as Jesus bugs because of their ability to walk on water.

Cockroaches

▲ *Cockroaches are not dirty creatures. They work hard to keep themselves clean in order to preserve a coating of wax and oils that prevents them from drying out. It is the bacteria they carry that makes them dangerous.*

- **Cockroaches belong** to the order Blattodea of class Insecta. There are about 4000 known species of cockroaches. Some well-known cockroaches are oriental black beetles and croton bugs.
- **Cockroaches are found** everywhere, especially in bat caves, peoples' homes, under stones, in thick grass and on trees and plants. The cockroaches found in caves are usually blind.
- **These insects** can be winged or wingless. Adult cockroaches can be 1 to 9 cm long. They are nocturnal and prefer dark and damp places.

- **Cockroaches are swift creatures** and can run extremely fast. Their legs are adapted for quick movement. They have flat and oval bodies that help them to hide in narrow cracks in walls and floors.
- **Most cockroach species** are omnivorous. Their main food is plant sap, dead animals and vegetable matter but they will even eat shoe polish, glue, soap and ink.
- **Adults can live** for up to two years. Males and females are very similar in appearance but males have a pair of bristle-like styli.
- **In some species**, females release pheromones or produce a hissing sound and wave their abdomen to attract male cockroaches.
- **Females can lay** up to 30 to 40 eggs at a time and can reproduce four times in a year. They store the eggs in a brownish egg case called an ootheca. The cockroach can either carry this egg case along with her or hide it somewhere. The young cockroaches are called nymphs.
- **Cockroaches** play an important role in balancing the environment by digesting a wide range of waste substances. They decompose forest and animal waste matter. At the same time, household cockroaches can contaminate food and spread diseases among humans.

...FASCINATING FACT...

The name cockroach comes from the Spanish word *cucaracha.* These insects adapt quickly to changes in the environment and can even survive a nuclear explosion.

Madagascan hissing cockroach

- **Madagascan hissing cockroaches** are found on the island of Madagascar, off the south-east coast of Africa. They are large, wingless insects, famous for the loud hissing sound that they make. These hisses are loud enough for people to hear.
- **These cockroaches** are chocolate brown in colour, with dark orange marks on their abdomen. Adults can grow up to 10 cm in length.

▼ *Hissing cockroaches make their distinctive noise by pushing air out of a pair of breathing holes in the side of their body. They have spiky legs for grip and protection.*

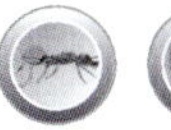

- **A male cockroach** can distinguish between familiar males and strangers from the hissing sound that they make.
- **Males** look different from the females. They have a large, hornlike structure behind their heads and are more aggressive than the females. They also have hairy antennae, unlike the smooth antennae of the females.
- **These cockroaches** feed on dead animal matter, waste food or ripe fruits.
- **Females** can produce 30 to 60 eggs that they store in an egg sac, either inside or outside their body. The eggs hatch into small nymphs.
- **The nymphs** of hissing cockroaches moult six times in a period of seven months before maturing into adult cockroaches. While moulting, the skin of a cockroach splits down the middle of its back and the cockroach slowly wriggles out.
- **Newly moulted cockroaches** are whitish but their colour darkens within a few hours. Hissing cockroaches can live for 2 to 5 years.
- **Madagascan hissing cockroaches** can be easily bred in homes and classrooms. For this reason, they are ideal for classroom study.

FASCINATING FACT

Male hissing cockroaches are territorial. They fight amongst themselves by ramming and pushing with their horns and abdomens. Once the fight is over, the winner makes loud hissing sounds to declare victory.

Oriental cockroach

- **Oriental cockroaches** are seasonal insects and can be most easily spotted during the spring and summer. They are found in places such as damp basements, drains, leaky pipes, and kitchen sinks.
- **These cockroaches** are dark brown or black in colour so they are sometimes called 'black beetles'. Adults can grow up to 3.5 cm in length.
- **This cockroach** is sometimes called the 'shad roach' because its young appear in large numbers when shad (a fish) are swimming into fresh waters to breed.
- **Males** have short wings but females are wingless.

- **Females** do have small wing stubs. This is what makes them different from their own nymphs.
- **A female** can produce 5 to 10 egg cases (oothecae) in her lifetime. Each egg case contains about ten eggs.
- **Young cockroach nymphs** hatch from the egg cases in 6 to 8 weeks and mature in 6 to 12 months. Adult cockroaches can live up to one year.
- **These cockroaches** can enter homes through sewer pipes, air ducts or any other opening.
- **Unlike other pest cockroaches**, oriental cockroaches do not have sticky pads on their feet and cannot climb slippery or smooth surfaces.

...FASCINATING FACT...
Oriental cockroaches can survive for up to a month without food, if water is available.

◀ *The head of this male oriental cockroach is almost hidden under the large hard collar (pronotum) at the front of the thorax. The cerci at the end of the abdomen are important sensory organs.*

Death's head cockroach

▲ *A fast runner, the death's head cockroach lives on the ground, searching through leaf litter or bat droppings for scraps of food.*

- **Death's head cockroaches** are large insects. They measure 5 to 8 cm in length. These cockroaches are mostly found in the Americas.
- **This cockroach** is named after the strange markings on its thorax. These markings look like skulls or vampires.
- **This insect** is also known as the palmetto bug or giant death's head cockroach.
- **Death's head cockroaches live mostly** in tropical forests or bat caves but sometimes, they are also found in buildings.
- **Death's head cockroaches** are brownish in colour with yellow and black marks on their body. While adults are beautifully coloured, the nymphs are dark in colour, although newly moulted nymphs are whitish.
- **The wings** are very long and cover their abdomen. The nymphs are wingless.
- **Females** carry the eggs inside their bodies and give birth to live young that hatch from the eggs.
- **Cockroaches** are scavengers and are active at night.
- **Decaying plant** and animal matter are the favourite food of these cockroaches.

...FASCINATING FACT...
Death's head cockroaches make good pets and are popular among cockroach lovers.

Crickets

- **Crickets belong** to the order Orthoptera and closely resemble grasshoppers. These insects are found almost everywhere – in fields, forests and gardens.
- **Crickets** have flattened bodies and long antennae and measure up to 5 cm. Although all crickets have wings, some species do not fly. They can only hop from one place to another.
- **These insects** make chirping sounds that attract females and warn rival males to keep away. The sounds may also act as warning signals.
- **Crickets** produce these sounds by rubbing the bases of their specially modified forewings.

▼ *Crickets hatch out into nymphs that look like miniature adults without wings. They go through up to ten or more moults as they develop into winged adults.*

- **Crickets are nocturnal** and have keen hearing and eyesight. Compound eyes help crickets see far and in many directions at the same time. Round, flat hearing organs are found on the front legs.
- **Crickets are omnivorous** and feed on crops, vegetables, flowers, green plants, small animals, clothes and each other.
- **Females** have long needle-like ovipositors to lay eggs. They carry the eggs until they find a safe place where the eggs can hatch into nymphs.
- **Some species** of crickets are considered to be pests because they can eat crops and deposit their eggs on them.
- **In some parts of the world**, crickets are thought to be a sign of good luck. For this reason, some people keep crickets as pets.

...FASCINATING FACT...

The ancient Chinese conducted 'cricket matches' in which crickets would wrestle with each other.

Cave cricket

- **Cave crickets are named** after their habit of living in caves and other dark and damp places.
- **These crickets** are also found in wells, rotten logs, hollow trees and under damp leaves and stones.

▼ *The long, sensitive antennae of the cave cricket help it to find its way around in the dark. The long cerci at the end of the abdomen also have a sensory function.*

- **These insects** are also known as cave crickets because they have a hump on their back.
- **Very long** hind legs give cave crickets a spider-like appearance. Their strong hind legs make them good jumpers.
- **Cave crickets are brown** in colour and have long antennae. They do not have wings.
- **These insects cannot chirp** or make sounds because they are wingless. Crickets normally produce a high-pitched sound by rubbing their wings together.
- **Cave crickets** are omnivorous and feed on decaying organic matter, plants and vegetables.
- **In the spring**, females lay their eggs in soil. The nymphs and adults spend the winter in sheltered areas.
- **Cave crickets** can damage articles stored in boxes, garages and laundry rooms, as they love to live in cool and damp places.
- **Cave crickets** are sometimes troublesome in buildings and homes, especially in basements.

Field cricket

▼ *The black antennae of the field cricket are longer than its body. It has shorter front wings thanthose of a grasshopper.*

- **Field crickets** are usually found in green fields and forested areas.
- **These insects** are either black or brown in colour and measure about 2.5 cm in length.
- **Spiky projections** called cerci can be found on their abdomen of field crickets.
- **Field crickets** are omnivorous and feed on plant seeds, smaller insects and fruits. Some species of field crickets become cannibalistic if there is a shortage of food.
- **Males** attract female crickets by chirping and dancing. They perform a courtship dance before mating. The high-pitched sounds they make are heard from early spring to autumn.
- **Females** usually lay about 50 eggs at a time. They can lay up to 400 eggs in their lifetime.
- **Eggs** are stored in the female's ovipositor until she finds damp soil, where the eggs are deposited.
- **Field crickets** do nut usually survive the winter, although their eggs can withstand harsh weather conditions.
- **Frogs**, birds and other insects feed on field crickets.
- **Field crickets** are very active at night.

Katydid

- **Katydids** are usually green-coloured insects. They are 5 to 6 cm in length and have two pairs of wings.
- **These insects** can be found in grasslands, fields and rainforests.
- **The eardrums** of katydids are located on their front legs.
- **Katydids** have long hind legs and antennae. Their antennae help them search for food. Their long back legs help them to make powerful jumps.
- **Katydids can fly** short distances and feed on willow leaves, rosewood and citrus trees.
- **The males** of various species produce different sounds to communicate with members of their own species and with males of other species.
- **Females** respond to mating calls by singing a soft 'song'.
- **The female lays her eggs** in bark, on twigs or on leaves. The eggs hatch into nymphs within three months. The total lifespan of katydids is about one year.
- **Katydids** are nocturnal insects.

...FASCINATING FACT...

Katydids are named after their loud calls that sound like 'Katy-did-Katy-didn't'.

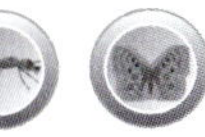

▼ *Katydids are well camouflaged as they rest among leaves during the day. Some tropical species even have fake leaf veins and chewed leaf edges to their wings to make them look even more like real leaves.*

Grasshoppers

- **Grasshoppers are green** or brown in colour. Some species change colours in different seasons. The body is divided into head, thorax and abdomen. They have six legs and a pair of compound eyes and wings.
- **Found almost everywhere** except in the polar regions, grasshoppers prefer to live in green fields, meadows and forest areas.
- **There are three main types** of grasshoppers – long-horned, short-horned and pygmy.

▶ *Grasshoppers have large, flat-sided heads with big compound eyes and sharp, biting jaws below the rest of the head. The antennae range in length from short to extremely long.*

FASCINATING FACT

When captured, grasshoppers spit a brown liquid to protect themselves from their predators. In some parts of the world, this brown liquid is known as tobacco juice.

▶ *When a grasshopper is at rest, the wide, delicate, back wings are folded like a fan underneath the long, narrow front wings. The front wings are lifted up to allow the flying wings to spread out when the grasshopper flies.*

- **Grasshoppers make** a loud noise during the mating season to attract a mate or scare away rivals.
- **After mating**, the female lays her eggs in low bushes or digs a hole in the soil with her abdomen to deposit eggs from her ovipositor. She covers her eggs with a hard shell covering called an egg-pod.
- **Grasshoppers are herbivorous**. They feed on a variety of plants, grasses and crops. They use their mandibles to chew food.
- **These insects** pose a serious threat to crops. A large group of grasshoppers can destroy an entire crop.
- **Flies, spiders, toads and reptiles** prey on grasshoppers and even eat their eggs.
- **In some parts of the world**, grasshoppers are considered a delicacy. They are ground into a meal, and sometimes fried or roasted and dipped in honey.

Bark bush cricket

- **Bark bush crickets** are so-called as they usually live on the bark of trees and shrubs in forests.
- **Bark bush crickets** have flat bodies. These insects are actually grasshoppers with long, threadlike antennae. For this reason, they are also known as long-horned grasshoppers.
- **These crickets are found** in different colours – from green to brown or even grey. They have underwings that are usually red and black in colour.
- **Bark bush crickets sing** at night and each species has a distinct song.
- **Bark bush crickets produce** a high-pitched chirping sound.
- **Unlike grasshoppers**, bark bush crickets produce sound by rubbing their forewings. Their ears are situated on their front legs.
- **Male bark bush crickets** are aggressive in nature and fiercely defend their territory.
- **The female** lays her eggs in the bark of trees, and leaf-stalks.
- **Sometimes,** when the eggs are laid in tissues of living plants, they are transported to other countries with the plants.
- **Unlike grasshoppers**, females do not cover their eggs with an egg-pod, which is a hard shell-like covering.

▼ *Most species of bark bush cricket are omnivorous and feed on leaves, flowers, fruits and other insects.*

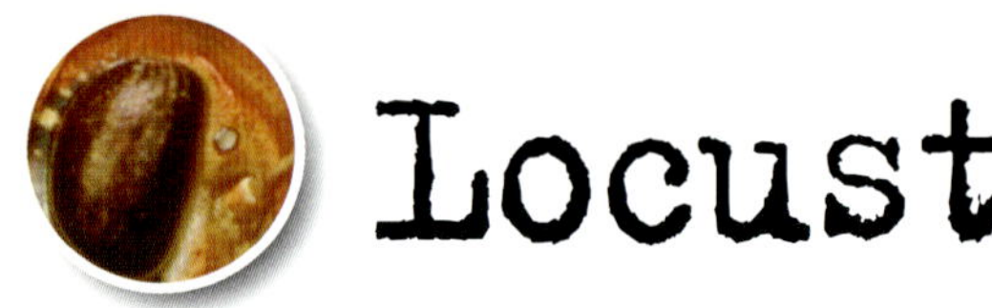

Locust

- **Locusts are found** all over the world except in cold regions. They are dark brown in colour and their average length is less than 2.5 cm.
- **Locusts live in** fields, open woods or arid areas.
- **These insects** are migratory in nature and can travel great distances. They can be highly destructive of crops. A large swarm can consume 3000 tons of green plants in a single day.
- **Locusts can breed** very quickly compared to other insects. Some well-known species are the desert locust, the red-legged locust and the Carolina locust.
- **Females** lay their eggs in the soil. The nymphs are wingless and small in size. A female locust can lay 20 eggs at a time.

▲ *A locust can use its powerful leg muscles to jump ten times its own body length.*

- **A locust** eats food equivalent to its own weight every day. It feeds on crops, weeds, grass or other plants.
- **Locusts have two phases** – solitary and gregarious. In the solitary phase, locusts do not breed in large numbers and confine themselves to their surroundings. In the second phase, the insect reproduces and grows quickly in the presence of an abundant food supply. This is known as the gregarious phase.

▲ *Locusts can fly for up to 20 hours using reserves of fat stored in their bodies.*

- **In the gregarious phase**, the locusts accumulate in large numbers. As a result, the habitat where they stay is not sufficient to support and sustain them. Therefore, these insects migrate in search of new feeding grounds and this phenomenon is called swarming.
- **In some** tribal groups, dried locusts are eaten as food.

FASCINATING FACT

A locust swarm may occupy 26 to 777 sq km. Such swarms cast a shadow on the ground and appear like a huge black cloud.

Stick insect

- **Stick insects belong** to the order Phasmatodea. They look like leafless sticks and branches and are also called walkingsticks.
- **These insects** are green or brown in colour and spend their time clinging to trees, plants and shrubs.
- **Stick insects are excellent** at camouflaging themselves, especially when they keep perfectly still or sway with the wind.

▼ *A stick insect has an extremely long, thin body, with threadlike antennae made up of as many as 100 segments. Some tropical stick insects grow as long as 30 cm, not including their legs or antennae. The giant stick insect from Indonesia is the longest of all insects.*

- **Some tropical species** of stick insect have sharp spines on their legs, which blend with the thorns of plants. If threatened, they can stab their enemies. They also change their colour like chameleons, depending on the humidity and temperature.

...FASCINATING FACT...

Stick insects lie motionless and pretend to be dead to save themselves from their predators. This is called catalepsis.

- **Stick insects are active at night**, when they feed on foliage.
- **Females** are larger than the males. Males can fly but the females can only glide.
- **Females produce** pheromones to attract males. A single female can lay about 1000 eggs in its lifetime. They scatter their eggs randomly or hide them in order to protect them.
- **Asiatic stick insects** are the longest stick insects, measuring more than 30 cm.
- **Stick insects** are the only insects that can regenerate lost legs. If old limbs are cut off they can grow new ones.

▲ *Stick insects have other means of defence as well as their excellent camouflage. If they are disturbed, they may suddenly drop to the ground or lose one of their legs to avoid capture. Many are wingless, but those with wings may flash their brightly coloured back wings to startle a predator.*

Leaf insect

- **Leaf insects belong** to the order Phasmatodea and are most common in south-east Asia.
- **These insects** have a unique appearance. Their bodies are flat, irregular in shape and resemble a leaf. These insects are about 10 cm in length and sometimes have brown or yellow patches on their body.

▲ *This leaf insect would be very hard for predators to spot among green leaves, as long as it remained completely still.*

...FASCINATING FACT...
Leaf insects are leafy green in colour and are popularly known as walking leaves.

- **Females** are much larger than males. They do not have hind wings and cannot fly but they have leaflike forewings.
- **The female can lay eggs** without mating with the male. This is called parthenogenesis.
- **A female** scatters her eggs on the ground. These eggs have a hard outer shell and resemble seeds, so predators do not feed on them.
- **The eggs** hatch in the spring.
- **Leaf insects are herbivorous** and feed only on green leaves and other parts of plants.
- **Rodents**, birds and other insects feed on leaf insects.
- **Leaf insects** are good at camouflage and hiding from predators. They move very slowly and mimic the foliage on which they live.

Damselfly

- **Damselflies** belong to the order Odonata and suborder Zygoptera. They have long, slender bodies and four long wings. They are weak fliers and timid predators.
- **These insects are beautiful**, slender cousins of dragonflies but are not as ferocious. They have compound eyes and excellent eyesight.
- **Damselflies** are usually found near water and their nymphs live in the water until they mature into adults.
- **Mosquitoes**, midgets, gnats and small water insects are the preferred food of damselflies.
- **Damselfly nymphs** have external gills on the tip of their abdomen for breathing underwater. In dragonfly nymphs, these gills are internal.
- **Males and females** mate during flight or over shallow water. While mating, a male carries a female around to allow her to collect sperm from the front of his abdomen.

...FASCINATING FACT...

Damselflies capture their prey with the help of their legs, folding them like a basket to form a trap. Once the insect is trapped it is transferred to the damselfly's mouth.

- **After mating**, females deposit their eggs in and around water.
- **The lifespan** of a damselfly is around one year but it can live up to two years.
- **During winter**, damselflies hibernate to survive the cold weather.

◀ *The large compound eyes of a damselfly bulge out to the side. Damselflies also have long legs, which they use to hold insects captured in flight. Their legs are not suited to walking.*

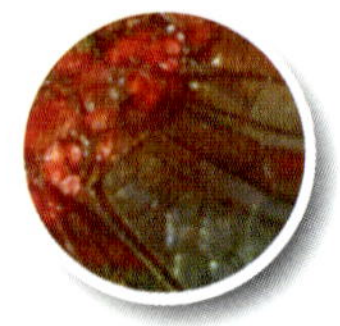

Dragonfly

- **Dragonflies are named** after their fierce jaws, which they use for catching prey.
- **These insects can grow up** to 12 cm in length. They have multi-coloured, long, slender bodies with two pairs of veined wings.
- **Larger dragonflies** are called hawkers while the smaller ones are called darters. Dragonflies have huge compound eyes, which cover the insect's entire head.
- **Adult dragonflies** survive on land but their nymphs live underwater. They cannot survive harsh winters.
- **The lifespan** of a dragonfly ranges from six months to more than seven years.

▶ *Each one of a dragonfly's wings can moves independently. This makes the dragonfly a very versatile flyer, able to hover, turn at 90 degree angles, dart backwards and forwards and come to a sudden stop.*

- **Males and females** mate while they fly. Once they have mated, the female dragonfly deposits her eggs in water or inside water plants.
- **A female dragonfly** lays up to 100,000 eggs at a time. These eggs hatch into nymphs. These nymphs feed on fish, tadpoles and other small aquatic animals.
- **Dragonflies** are beneficial to humans. They prey on mosquitoes, flies and many small insects that are pests.
- **Experts** have found dragonfly fossils that are more than 300 million years old. These prehistoric dragonflies were as big as crows.

FASCINATING FACT

Dragonflies are one of the fastest insects. They can fly at 30 to 50 km/h. The design and mechanism of a helicopter was probably inspired by a dragonfly.

Praying mantis

- **Praying mantises** belong to the order Mantodea. These insects are closely related to cockroaches.
- **The praying mantis** gets its name from its posture. This insect holds its front legs together as if it were praying.
- **These insect**s can grow up to 6.5 cm in length. They have triangular heads that can turn in a full circle. They are generally green or brown in colour.
- **Praying mantises have good** camouflage to protect themselves from predators. Their body colour blends with their environment. A species called the Asiatic rose mantis, even looks like flower petals. For this reason, it is also called the orchid mantis.
- **Females** are larger than the males. They lay their eggs inside an egg case (ootheca) during the autumn.
- **Females secrete** a sticky substance to stick their eggs to plant stems and tree twigs. Nymphs hatch from these eggs in the spring or summer.
- **Praying mantises** are carnivorous and feed on insects, such as butterflies, moths and grasshoppers. They can even attack small lizards, frogs and birds. Small mantises can become cannibalistic, especially when there is no food.
- **While feeding**, a praying mantis holds its prey with its front legs. It has a habit of silently watching and stalking its prey before attacking.
- **Praying mantises are useful** to humans. They protect crops by feeding on pests. Sometimes farmers buy them for pest control. These insects are often kept as pets, even though large praying mantises can hurt people.

▲ *A praying mantis moves its long front legs very rapidly to grab its prey. Sharp spines stop the prey from escaping. The mantis bites deeply into its victims with its powerful jaws.*

...FASCINATING FACT...

A female praying mantis often eats the male while mating!

Lacewing

- **Lacewings** are delicate green or brown insect which are named after their thin, translucent, lacelike wings.
- **These insects have long**, threadlike antennae and their eyes are bright golden yellow or brown in colour.
- **Birds and other predators** avoid lacewings because they give off a pungent odour similar to garlic.
- **Lacewings are not good fliers** because their wings are too weak to support their weight for long distances. These insects are often seen fluttering about clumsily.

▼ *A lacewing has two similar pairs of wings, which are covered with a delicate network of veins. When the lacewing rests, it holds its wings together like a roof over its body.*

- **A lacewing lays** a large number of eggs at a time. The eggs are white in colour and are glued to a twig or leaf. Green lacewings secrete a thin white stalk for each egg.
- **Lacewing larvae** feed on small insects. They eat a lot of aphids (greenfly) in a day and are also known as aphid lions. These insects are sometimes used to control the population of aphids in crop fields.
- **The larvae of lacewings** are sometimes reared commercially to get rid of pests. Apart from aphids, these larvae feed on pests, such as mealybugs, leafhoppers, caterpillars, moths and other insects. The larvae can become cannibalistic if there is not enough food to go around.
- **Lacewing larvae** have 'jaws', which make them resemble alligators. They are used to suck the body fluids of the prey after injecting it with paralyzing venom.
- **Some lacewing larvae** camouflage themselves with debris, including the skin and other remains of their prey.
- **Many species of adult lacewings** do not eat other insects. Instead, they feed on nectar, pollen and honeydew.

Mantisfly

◀ *A mantisfly grabs its prey with its huge front legs. The wings of a mantisfly are very different from those of a praying mantis* *(see page 193)*.

- **Mantisflies are named** after their folded pair of front legs, which look like those of praying mantises. Although these insects look similar, they are not related.
- **These insects** are not common and are found in tropical regions.
- **Mantisflies**, along with lacewings and antlions, belong to the order Neuroptera.
- **Mantisflies lay** their rose-coloured eggs on slender plant stalks.
- **The mantisfly** has a complicated development cycle. It has two growth stages as a larva and two more stages as a pupa.
- **The larva** of one species of mantisfly is a parasite of wolf spiders. A single larva enters a cocoon and preys upon the egg or young. The larva pierces the egg or spider with its pointed mouthparts and feeds on its body fluids.
- **The larva** then pupates inside the spider's cocoon.
- **The parent spider** watches over the cocoon, unaware of the presence of the parasite mantisfly.
- **Some mantisflies mimic** wasps and bees for protection.
- **Mantisflies** are as predatory as praying mantises and have similar feeding habits.

Antlion

▶ *The stout, clubbed antennae of adult antlions are very different from the short, thin antennae of dragonflies (see page 190).*

- **Antlions are named** after the larva's habit of feeding on ants and other insects. Adult antlions feed on pollen or nectar or do not feed at all.
- **Antlions resemble dragonflies.** They both have long slender bodies and four delicate wings. However, unlike dragonflies, antlions are nocturnal in nature.
- **These insects** are found in damp areas where vegetation is thick. Antlions are also found near riverbeds.
- **Some antlion larvae** make a pit in the sand by moving around in a spiral path and throwing out sand.
- **While making the pit**, the larva leaves behind squiggly doodles on the sand. For this reason, antlions are also known as doodlebugs.
- **The larva** then waits inside the pit and feeds on insects that fall into it. When the prey struggles to escape, the larva throws sand on it to make it fall back down into the pit.

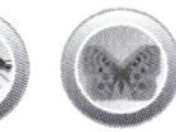

- **Once the larva** has sucked the body juices of its victim, the remains of the insect are thrown out of the pit. These larvae are voracious eaters and can eat even adult antlions when food is scarce.
- **An antlion larva secretes** silk and pupates inside a cocoon made of soil and silk.
- **Unlike the larva of other insects**, an antlion larva secretes silk from the tip of its abdomen instead of its mouth.

▲ *An antlion larva waits at the bottom of its pit trap for an unsuspecting insect to fall down into its pincer-like jaws.*

FASCINATING FACT

Antlion larvae have a peculiar appearance. Their shape has inspired the creation of monsters in many Hollywood science fiction movies.

Stonefly

▶ *The flattened body of a stonefly nymph helps to stop it being washed away as it clings to stones at the bottom of streams. It has only two cerci at the tip of its abdomen, whereas mayfly nymphs have three of these sensory structures.*

- **Stoneflies** are an ancient order of insects which has been around for nearly 300 million years.
- **Stonefly** nymphs cling to stones in clear mountain streams or lakes. They are eaten by fish and are also used as models for artificial fish bait.
- **Some stonefly nymphs** breathe through gills, which are present near their legs. Others obtain oxygen through their body surface.

- **Adult stoneflies are terrestrial,** which means that they live on land. However, they never wander too far from water, spending their time crawling over stones. This is how their name originates.
- **Female stoneflies** deposit their eggs in deep water. To prevent the eggs from floating away, they stick them to rocks with a sticky secretion.

...FASCINATING FACT...
Some male stoneflies attract the females by drumming their abdomen against a hard surface. These insects are popularly known as 'primitive drummers' for this reason.

- **A stonefly nymph** resembles an adult but does not have wings and its reproductive organs are not as well developed. These nymphs grow into adult stoneflies and crawl out of the water. A stonefly lives for up to two to three years.
- **Stonefly nymphs feed** on underwater plants, such as algae and lichens. Some species are carnivorous and feed on aquatic insects. Adults may not feed at all, although some feed on algae and pollen.
- **Fishes** often attack female stoneflies when they try to deposit their eggs in streams.
- **Stoneflies are sensitive** to water pollution. Experts use these insects to study the level of water purity.

Scorpionfly

- **Scorpionflies** are a small group of insects with dark spots on their two pairs of membranous wings. These primitive insects have been around for 250 million years.
- **The rear body part** of some males is curled upwards, similar to a scorpion's. Only males resemble scorpions.

▼ *The most distinctive feature of scorpionflies is their elongated head with a long 'beak', which ends in biting jaws. This one does not have the scorpion-like tail.*

- **Adult scorpionflies** have modified mouthparts. They have a long beak pointing downwards.
- **Scorpionflies feed** on live as well as dead insects. Some also feed on pollen, nectar and plants.
- **They are predators** and often steal their food from spiders' webs. Scorpionflies catch their prey with their hind legs.
- **While mating**, a male scorpionfly secretes a sweet, sticky secretion, on which the female scorpionfly feeds.
- **A female scorpionfly** lays her eggs in wooden crevices and soil. The eggs hatch and the larvae live and pupate in loose soil or waste material.
- **Scorpionfly larvae feed** on dead and rotten plant and animal matter. Some larvae also feed on small insects.
- **Scorpionflies** are often considered helpful to humans because they keep the environment clean by feeding on dead insects.

...FASCINATING FACT...

During the mating season, a male scorpionfly offers the female a gift. This courtship gift can be a dead insect or a drop of his saliva.

Silverfish

- **The silverfish** is a primitive insect, which belongs to the order Thysanura.
- **These insects** are soft-bodied and do not have wings. Silverfishes have a longish body with three tail filaments.
- **Silverfishes** are silver or brown in colour and can move very swiftly.

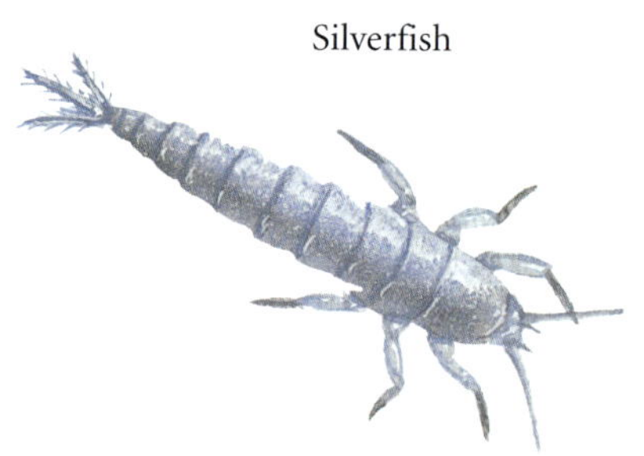

Silverfish

- **Silverfishes prefer to live in** places that are dark and very humid. They are mostly found in moist and warm places, such as kitchens and baths.
- **These insects generally feed** on flour, glue, paper, leftover food and even clothes. Silverfishes can easily survive for months without food.
- **Silverfishes mate** in a unique manner. A male spins a silk thread and deposits his sperm on it. The female then comes near this thread, picks up the sperm and uses it to fertilize her eggs.
- **A female silverfish** can lay up to 100 eggs in her lifetime. After mating, she deposits clusters of her eggs in cracks or crevices.
- **Even after** maturing into adults, these insects continue to moult. They can live for two to eight years.
- **Generally harmless** to humans, silverfishes but they can contaminate food.
- **Silverfishes can destroy** books and are considered indoor pests.

▲ *Silverfish are named after the tiny, shiny scales that cover their carrot-shaped body (bottom right). They belong to a group of insects called bristletails because their abdomen ends in a central tail, which is fringed with bristles.*

Springtail

- **Springtails** belong to the order Collembola.
- **Springtails are wingless** insects measuring up to 1 to 5 mm in length. Unlike most other insects, springtails do not have compound eyes.
- **These insects** have a springlike organ, known as a furcula, under their abdomen. It helps them to leap high into the air.
- **Springtails** do not have a respiratory system. They breathe through their cuticle (hard skin).
- **Even though** springtails can jump, they normally crawl from one place to another.
- **Springtails prefer** to live in soil and moist habitats. However they can survive almost anywhere in the world including Antarctica and Arctic regions.
- **Decaying vegetable matter**, pollen, algae and other plants are the preferred food of springtails.
- **A female springtail** lays approximately 90 to 150 eggs in her lifetime.
- **The lifespan** of a springtail is one year or less.

...FASCINATING FACT...

Springtails are also called snow fleas as they can survive in extreme cold. They are active even in freezing weather.

▲ *Springtails have to live in moist places because their bodies dry out easily. They are usually a grey or brown colour, sometimes with mottled colours for camouflage.*

Index

A

Index

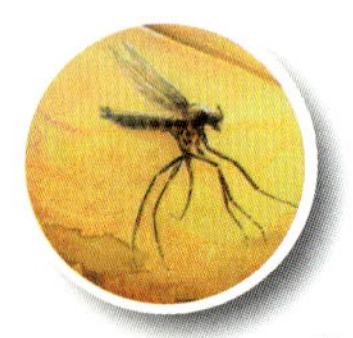

Index

Index

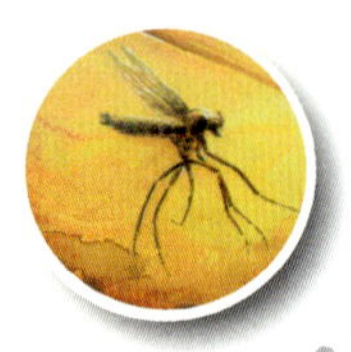

Index

M

Index

Q

R

Index

Acknowledgements

All artworks are from Miles Kelly Artwork Bank

All other photographs from:

Castrol
CMCD
Corbis
Corel
digitalSTOCK
digitalvision
Flat Earth
Hemera
ILN
John Foxx
PhotoAlto
PhotoDisc
PhotoEssentials
PhotoPro
Stockbyte